"Carlene Hill Byron wants the ch[...] whole lot of us sitting in the pews [...] challenges. Her decades-long expe[...] as a mental health advocate, and h[...] [...] researcher combine to make her book a gift to the church. Her practical, accessible writing equips church members and leaders to fully welcome and support the many in their midst who are facing mental health challenges. Her warmth, insight, and call to mature faithfulness will encourage every one of us to be more fully present in community, just as we are, even when we're not quite fine."

—**MICHELLE VAN LOON**, author of seven books, including the forthcoming *Translating Your Past: Finding Meaning in Family Ancestry, Genetic Clues, and Generational Trauma*

"The church should be a place of love and support for anyone struggling with mental health challenges, but anyone who has ever struggled with mental health problems—or walked alongside someone who has—knows that is too often not the case. In this much-needed book, Carlene Hill Byron gets to the roots of the problem and offers a hopeful vision for the church to take up the mantle of love by stepping into difficult places to come alongside those who are struggling. *Not Quite Fine* is a valuable resource for anyone who wants to transform the church into a place known for the kind of love and support we all so desperately need."

—**HAROLD G. KOENIG**, director of the Center for Spirituality, Theology and Health at Duke University Medical Center

"I will keep this book readily available for the rest of my life—for my mental health and the mental health of others! Carlene Hill Byron writes with enticing beauty supported with facts and evidence. You will get value from reading it for minutes or hours. The text is full of wisdom for anyone who cares for or about those who struggle. Since childhood, my life has included days when I want to go to bed and never wake up. This book will help."

—**BARBARA HEMPHILL**, founder of Productive Environment Institute

"Carlene Hill Byron brings the skill of an educator, the passion of an advocate, and the grounded wisdom of someone who lives with mental illness to offer a wise, poignant, and immensely practical guide to all who seek to ameliorate the mental health crisis that surrounds us. Christians, she writes, are called to refuse the individualism and perfectionism in our culture that intensify mental health challenges, and instead are to cultivate—humbly and without fear—communities of patience, purpose, and belonging. For those who care about mental illness and wonder how to help, this is a wonderful place to start."

—**WARREN KINGHORN, MD, ThD**, Duke University Medical Center and Duke Divinity School

"*Not Quite Fine* is timely and practical. It informs the reader with an engaging answer to the question, Where is it safe to suffer? It challenged me to think through mental health issues, and it is a compelling book for friends and other loved ones. Carlene Hill Byron takes her personal story and engages the reader with cultural relevance, providing a road map to bridge the gap between mental health and the church. *Not Quite Fine* is a must-read, must-think-about, and must-share with people. It is a great asset in your journey toward flourishing."

—**WENDY CLARK**, CEO and founder of the Durham Exchange

NOT

QUITE

FINE

CARLENE HILL BYRON

NOT QUITE FINE

*Mental Health, Faith, and
Showing Up for One Another*

HERALD
PRESS

Harrisonburg, Virginia

Herald Press
PO Box 866, Harrisonburg, Virginia 22803
www.HeraldPress.com

Library of Congress Cataloging-in-Publication Data
Names: Byron, Carlene Hill, author.
Title: Not quite fine : mental health, faith, and showing up for one
    another / Carlene Hill Byron.
Description: Harrisonburg, Virginia : Herald Press, 2021. | Includes
    bibliographical references.
Identifiers: LCCN 2021025712 (print) | LCCN 2021025713 (ebook) | ISBN
    9781513808215 (paperback) | ISBN 9781513808222 (hardcover) | ISBN
    9781513808239 (ebook)
Subjects: LCSH: Church work with the mentally ill. | Pastoral psychology. |
    Mentally ill--Pastoral counseling of. | BISAC: RELIGION / Christian
    Ministry / Counseling & Recovery | PSYCHOLOGY / Psychopathology /
    General
Classification: LCC BV4461 .B97 2021 (print) | LCC BV4461 (ebook) | DDC
    259/.42--dcundefined
LC record available at https://lccn.loc.gov/2021025712
LC ebook record available at https://lccn.loc.gov/2021025713

Study guides are available for many Herald Press titles at www.HeraldPress.com.

25 24 23 22 21   10 9 8 7 6 5 4 3 2 1

To all the people of God
who know they're "not quite fine"
but don't know who to talk with.

To all the people of God
who can see someone's "not quite fine"
but don't know how to talk about it.

Together, let's walk into our calling
for "such a time as this."

Contents

Foreword

In the United States as well as in other parts of the world, deaths of despair continue to climb, despite the widespread use of psychiatric diagnosis and medication—an indication that reductions in stigma and improved treatments are outmatched by the pervasive, deleterious impacts of social dislocation.

Communities of faith remain the first place many people go for help with emotional struggles. While congregations represent potential sources of understanding, connection, and inspiration, members and leaders often feel ill-equipped to handle the challenges that suffering individuals present, and thus feel uncomfortable or fearful of embracing them.

Professionals such as psychiatrist Dan Blazer and theologian John Swinton have called attention to what a Christian community can offer those with mental health challenges. But the voices of these individuals and of church members trying to help them are too seldom heard. This is what makes *Not Quite Fine* such a valuable contribution. Using her own experience with bipolar disorder and suicidal ideation, as well as what she has learned from the lived experience of others, author Carlene Hill Byron explains in practical terms how fellow believers can help those who suffer continue to find in their faith meaning, purpose, belonging, value, and hope. While congregation members may not (and generally should not) provide professional care, they can provide what is at least as important—companionship and support that connects struggling individuals with a God who loves them. As a believing psychiatrist, I find the wisdom and clarity of Byron's message to be very welcome and deeply encouraging.

—John R. Peteet, MD
    associate professor of psychiatry at Harvard
    Medical School and staff psychiatrist at Brigham
    and Women's Hospital and Dana-Farber Cancer
    Institute

Introduction

My personal mental health journey began more than forty-five years ago, when I first walked into a counselor's office at my college. Within two years, another counselor would assign my first diagnosis and send me to a psychiatrist for my first prescription.

Since then, I've had five different diagnoses and been prescribed twenty-two different psychiatric medications. Psychiatry has been a rapidly changing field: My first diagnosis no longer exists. My second was replaced when I alerted my doctor to symptoms that had been overlooked. My third was overturned when a different medication routine created symptoms of a different disorder. Attempts to treat that fourth diagnosis took me through more than fifteen medications in combinations of as many as five at a time over seven years. Diagnosis five was apparently assigned by my general practitioner—she logged it in her treatment report, which I read in the hospital's online patient portal.

My efforts to find and follow the best current mental health treatments have carried me through more than four decades of change. I've experienced philosophical changes in the mental health field, short-term changes in my life from new medicines, and changes that have had a longer impact on both my mental and physical health. Some were for the better. Others not so much.

Through all these changes, God is the same. Through all these changes, God's call to God's people is the same. And happily, congregations are still very often the first place where people in the United States go in times of emotional distress, even distress so serious we might call it "mental illness."

A GROWING MENTAL HEALTH CRISIS

I started writing this book just days before the COVID-19 pandemic locked down my part of the United States. Within weeks, mental health experts were describing a parallel pandemic of loneliness and anxiety. We were losing the touchstones of our normal lives, and it frightened us. We couldn't see the people we love . . . not even the people we used to pass in the park. Ordinary goals seemed unattainable at first, then began dropping out of view. Some people slid into a parallel universe of Netflix and snack food; others created a parallel universe of new hobbies and activities. First-time bakers stripped supermarket shelves of flour. Long daily walks gained traction as a lifestyle. Pastimes like origami and paint-by-number enjoyed a surprising renaissance as people sought ways to refocus and forget.

Now, as I finish this book more than a year later, the anticipated surge in COVID-related mental health problems has yet to subside. Therapy offices are overwhelmed. Many are turning away new patients because all their appointments are filled by current and returning clients. Online therapists, hotlines, warmlines (non-emergency support telephone services), and text services are the busiest they've ever been as they support people who never before felt a need to call a stranger for help.

Even before COVID-19 emerged as a deadly pandemic illness, American public health officials had already named a fatal mental health epidemic that was well underway: "deaths of despair." This statistical category encompasses two separate causes of death in the national mortality tables: deaths by suicide and deaths by drug overdose. Suicide deaths, on the rise since the 1990s, hit "top ten" killer status in the United States in 2008 and have remained stubbornly at this level since, accounting for about 47,000 deaths per year. Drug overdose deaths have also risen over that time, topping 87,000 in the most recently documented twelve-month period in the United States.[1] Opioid painkiller overdoses have been most often in the headlines, but certain psychiatric medicines are also associated with about two in ten overdose deaths. The introduction of this "deaths of despair" category reflects a growing awareness by public health officials that these deaths by suicide and overdose are related by the sense of hopelessness that drives them.

GOD'S CALL TO THE CHURCH IN MENTAL HEALTH CRISIS TIMES

The phrase "deaths of despair" cries out for intervention by the people of a loving God. If God has given us a hope that allows us to continue through our sufferings, surely we can walk with others whose view of hope has been obscured. And happily, as already mentioned, congregations are still a place where people in the United States are very likely to go first in times of emotional distress.

The faith community can—and should—help promote healthier mental states in all of us, including those who are struggling with mental health challenges. We know that God walks with each person along difficult paths, and that God is at the end of each person's path out of despair. We also know that God sets everyone's path and everyone's time. Because we are called by God, we are able to live with *meaning* and *purpose*. We can recognize we have *value* to God and in God's world. We know that we *belong* in God's family—a family that extends across miles and millennia. And we are able to have *hope*: hope for our own lives and times, and hope for the time that is to come.

As Christians, our framework for understanding human suffering doesn't exclude biological causes and influences on mental health, but it also doesn't give biology primary authority over human lives. To do that would be, in the words of mental health author Amy Simpson, to "believe brain cells are more powerful and more important than the One who made them."[2] Nor does our framework for Christian caring limit us to the kinds of care that meet biological needs. Those who work in medical professions have that expertise and deservedly hold authority in that arena. The rest of us are, for the most part, inexpert in biochemistry by God's choice and God's calling on our lives. God is, however, training all of us followers to be more expert in Christian living. The more our lives reflect Christ, the more we learn the human and spiritual skills of friendship and caring, the more we become agents of positive change in the lives of those with mental health problems.

As part of God's church, you can be part of God's system to support those who live with mental health problems. As you learn to observe the meaning, purpose, and value God recognizes in all created lives, you become increasingly skilled in helping others see what God sees in them. As you learn to welcome those who are sometimes too different to be readily understood, you will help them discover their own place of belonging in God's body. And as you listen closely to their stories and their dreams, you will help them find the sources of hope that God has built into their lives.

God has already begun preparing you, as a member of the body of Christ, to help people with mental health problems. God empowers every member of the body to offer meaning, purpose, belonging, value, and hope to those who need them. At various times, "those who need them" will include all our neighbors, those with and those without mental health challenges.

God designed the body of Christ to be an organism that hurts when any of its members hurt. God also empowered the body of Christ to be a healing community for members in pain—a place where feeble knees would be strengthened, if not healed in this lifetime, and where those who mourn would be raised up as rebuilders of the cities left in ruins.

Medicines and therapies have their roles in the support of people like me, who live with diagnosed mental illnesses. But God's own body, led by God's own Son, is intended to be the greatest support God has given us in this world. The right functioning of God's body requires every member be "joined and held together by every supporting ligament" so that God's life on earth "grows and builds itself up in love, as each part does its work" (Ephesians 4:16).

Those outside the United States will recognize that international perpectives significantly influence this book's approach to mental health. Global differences in mental health outcomes jumped into startling view for me when I began researching suicide prevention strategies for a conference talk over half a decade ago.[3] I discovered that suicide rates were dropping in most of the world while US rates continued to rise. I also found that successful prevention strategies often focused on social causes of suicide, such as joblessness or household debt, instead of attributing suicide to an individual's mental health problems. Global sources also raised questions for me about ways that wealthy Western cultures might be undermining mental health by creating the conditions in which anxiety and depression grow and by nurturing in people the belief that we suffer from unusually poor mental health rather than suffering under particularly difficult circumstances.

This book is designed to help you think about how you might participate in the supportive work that builds up entire communities, and in particular the entire body of Christ: those of us with diagnosed mental illnesses, those of us with mental health problems, and everyone else who belongs to the family of God. Our needs and callings are more alike than you may expect. In each chapter, you'll find sections that describe small beginnings that individuals and congregations may take, one particular challenge we face, and hopeful good news as we take on this work. Above all, this is a book about life walked side by side in Christ with people who experience great difficulties. When all the people of God choose to follow God together, we have truly chosen life as God has promised it. We gain blessings, not curses, and practice obedience, not willfulness, in the constant presence of our loving God who becomes our life (Deuteronomy 30:19-20).

A WORD ABOUT LANGUAGE

The term *mental illness* is not one I use by preference. It is used in this book as a historic term, in citations, and when describing formal diagnoses or diagnostic systems. Several considerations inform my preference for the term *mental health problems*:

- Mental health problems are quite common. If the coronavirus pandemic taught us nothing else, it taught us that a very large portion of us will experience emotional difficulties under difficult circumstances. Chapter 1 asks why the label "mental illness" is applied to so many emotional difficulties in the United States, and whether it's really appropriate for half of us to be ascribed this label in our lifetime, as has been predicted by the Centers for Disease Control and Prevention.

- To the extent that mental health problems represent common ways we respond to our circumstances, many effective mental health supports will simply help us change our circumstances (where that's possible), respond more effectively, or live with our suffering (for example, during the early months of grief). Chapter 3 begins the conversation about how nonprofessional supporters can aid those with mental health problems.

- To the extent that mental health problems reflect our cultural environment, calling them "mental illnesses" may not be helpful. During the early months of COVID-19, many understood quarantine-induced isolation as the catalyst for secondary epidemics of depression and anxiety. A different framing might describe those tides of anxiety and depression as growing symptoms of a long-standing cultural epidemic of loneliness that was made much worse by the mandated isolation many faced during the pandemic. Chapter 2 briefly reviews some international research relating loneliness to symptoms of mental illness, and what this implies about best approaches to care.

- When long stretches of hard times have skewed a person's biochemistry, the remedies that restore the person's physical health may not all be medicines. The scientific evidence base recognizes the value of such simple activities as gardening, dancing, walking in nature, establishing reliable routines, and talking with another person. These kinds of remedies don't require professional guidance, but they may be best supported with the side-by-side encouragement of a Christian friend.

Some people will find the pronouns in this book confusing. In the text, those with mental health problems are sometimes labeled "we" and sometimes, when described as recipients of care, "they." Those who care for people with mental health problems are sometimes called "they" and sometimes "we." And then, of course, there are times when "I" describes either a challenged individual or a caregiver, because I live both roles.

This attempt to acknowledge the many roles that each of us may fill can be confusing in print. But it is very encouraging in the life of God's people. All are called and gifted, and all face the limits of an imperfect world. Together, this means that all will both serve and be served. All face challenges, and God encourages us to live toward the time when all may overcome. I encourage patience in the reading, faithfulness in the living, and hope in our empowering God.

1

How Can the Mental Health Problem Have Gotten So Big, So Fast?

Orchids are not broken dandelions.

—**W. THOMAS BOYCE**, *The Orchid and the Dandelion*

When I began writing about mental health over a decade ago, statistics indicated that one in four households would be affected by mental health problems, at least in the person of some friend or relative. Today, the Centers for Disease Control and Prevention suggest that half of all Americans will be diagnosable with a mental illness in their lifetime.[1] More than one in six of us takes a prescribed psychiatric medication.[2] Then, in 2020, the coronavirus pandemic brought a new set of mental health concerns. Starting in the early days of the pandemic, mental health experts issued many cautions in the media about the mental illness pandemic they said was surging along with the viral disease. They feared that rising anxiety and depression would produce a dangerous secondary pandemic of suicides if not proactively contained.

Our conversation in the United States today suggests that we are living through a growing mental health crisis. But what if the crisis is less about our health and more about how we think about it? What if we've so dramatically changed our expectations about mental health that most of us can't meet the new norm?

HOW BIG IS THE MENTAL HEALTH PROBLEM?

It's not been long since mental illness was considered rare and even shameful. People with mental health problems were hidden away in asylums and never spoken of. They were like my mother's aunt Bessie, whose name I saw for the first time in an obituary at my late parents' home. It turns out that Bessie died in our state psychiatric hospital. Two copies of a family photograph poignantly tell her story. One shows the young woman Bessie laughing between her two brothers on our farmhouse's granite stoop. The other—well, it's no longer a full photograph. There's a slice of my grandfather Carl. A slice of my mother's uncle Percy. The section where Bessie appeared has been cut out.

In those days, only a tiny portion of the population was considered mentally ill. Between 1940 and 1950, public and private hospitals provided long-term homes to less than one-half of 1 percent of the population[3]—people like Aunt Bessie. Other people with mental health problems might be considered odd, soft-hearted, selfish, weepy, abusive, alcoholic, or idiosyncratic. But not mentally ill.

In less than three generations, the proportion of the US public that is professionally treated for mental health problems has risen dramatically. In the mid-1950s, the first mass-market prescription psychiatric drug, the sedative Miltown, was created. Within two years of its introduction, about one in twenty American adults[4] was taking what was popularly known as "executive Excedrin." Through the 1970s and 1980s, other new medications entered the market for the general public. Benzodiazepine drugs for anxiety, including Valium, were at the top of every "most frequently prescribed" list by the mid-1970s.[5] Over the next three decades, depression replaced anxiety as the most typical diagnosis,[6] and new classes of medications addressed what was then believed to be a depression-inducing shortage of a particular chemical transmitter in the brain.[7] Between 1990 and 1992, 12.2 percent of US adults ages eighteen to fifty-four received some kind of mental health treatment.[8] By 2019, nearly 20 percent of us were receiving some kind of mental health treatment and 15.8 percent of American adults were taking a psychiatric medication.[9]

Unfortunately, while more people are receiving mental health care, mental health in the United States does not appear to be improving. Just as access to and utilization of professional mental health treatments has increased, so also have the most serious consequences of mental health problems. Between 1999 and 2018, the rate of death by suicide in the United States increased by 35 percent.[10] Suicide deaths now exceed 48,000 per year, according to the Centers for Disease Control and Prevention.[11] Between 1990 and 2010, drug overdose death rates more than tripled,[12] and in the most recently recorded twelve-month period, more than 87,000 people in the United States died because of an overdose.[13] Most involve prescription medicines (typically opioid painkillers); as recently as 2017 more than one-fifth also involved prescription psychiatric medications (usually benzodiazepines).[14]

Both suicides and overdose deaths—now described together as "deaths of despair"—consistently rank among the top ten causes of death in US mortality tables. Suicide has remained stubbornly among the top ten causes of death in the United States for more than a decade, even while suicide deaths are declining in the rest of the world.

Why have mental health problems—including such serious mental health problems—become an increasingly large part of our American life?

NOT "NORMAL"? OR "NOT QUITE FINE"?

One reason we might consider mental illness to be more prevalent is because we now describe more human experiences as mental illnesses. If half of us will experience a mental illness during our lifetime, then it's normal (in the sense of "ordinary") to have what we now call a mental illness. And if half of us will experience a "mental illness" in our lifetime, then perhaps all we are saying is that half of us will be, at some time, less mentally healthy than the other half. That sounds more like math than diagnosis.

It's also possible that more people are diagnosed with mental illnesses because we have more diagnoses available. Mental health problems are described for practitioners in a volume called the *Diagnostic and Statistical Manual of Mental Disorders* (commonly abbreviated *DSM*). The first *DSM*, published in 1952 by the American Psychiatric Association, described symptoms of 128 different diagnoses in a 132-page book. The most recent edition, *DSM-5*, published in 2013, offers 541 diagnostic categories in its 947 pages. Some of the newer categories describe what previously would have been considered difficult human experiences once managed in churches, families, and communities—for example, an unwanted pregnancy or difficulties adjusting to a new culture. Naming and categorizing them makes it possible for providers to bill insurers when supporting people dealing with these circumstances. It also makes it more likely that we will consider these experiences to be serious conditions, even illnesses, that require professional care. After all, there are diagnostic codes for them!

MEDICAL STUDENT SYNDROME AND THE FOCUSING ILLUSION

Because advertising and educational campaigns have made all of us more knowledgeable about mental illness symptoms, we are also more likely to give diagnostic labels to our difficult feelings. A friend thought she might have "had anxiety" for some sleepless weeks as COVID-19 eroded the financial foundations of the organization where she was a manager. But was her anxiety an illness? Or was it a normal human response to a very stressful event?

One way to think about that question is by looking at another health condition, medical student syndrome. Medical student syndrome is the tendency among those preparing to become doctors to see in themselves whatever illness is being studied. Researchers find medical student syndrome afflicts as many as four in five people preparing to become physicians.[15] Medical students have to spend a lot of time thinking about illnesses. As they pay close attention to the lists of symptoms they are learning, they tend to see—and then magnify into a diagnosis—anything in their own lives that looks like a symptom.

Likewise, it's easy to magnify our own mental health problems into symptom-driven amateur diagnoses. Like the medical student memorizing her long lists of symptoms, we also carry in our minds an ever-growing list of warning signals for an ever-growing list of mental illnesses. Hundreds of head-lines, posts, and bulletins alert us to a rising tide of mental illnesses and remind us that these illnesses are the proper province of trained professional caregivers. And so when we insist on arranging our socks just so in the drawer, we (or our spouse) ask, "Isn't that kind of OCD?"[16] When we feel hopeless because making plans seems impossible in a COVID world, we ask, "Do I have depression?"

Very often, a person who sees in their life symptoms of mental illness is actually experiencing a form of suffering that finds its roots in culture, in circumstance, in consequences of their own actions, in the real experiences of real life in a fallen world. These forms of suffering are not illness. They are ordi-nary. We won't get better when we treat them inappropriately.

RAISING THE BAR ON "NORMAL" MENTAL HEALTH

We understand that to be "mentally ill" is to vary from some standard of mental health. Easy enough. But what is an appro-priate standard of mental health?

The World Health Organization (WHO) describes mental health as "a state of well-being in which the individual real-izes his or her own abilities, can cope with the normal stresses of life, can work productively and fruitfully, and is able to make a contribution to his or her community."[17] The *DSM* in many ways follows suit, often defining the difference between an ordinary emotional state and a diagnosable condition as whether the condition impedes ordinary functioning.

But what are the "normal stresses of life"? What is "ordi-nary functioning"?

Ordinary is always whatever is expected or allowable in a given time or place. That means that changing cultural norms can redefine what was once normal as mental illness.

How we think about grief in the United States is a good example. In nineteenth-century America, mourning the loss of a loved one involved a public ritual of wearing a dark color—black, gray, or purple—for up to a year. Even into the late twentieth century, grief was widely understood to be a long and painful experience. Hospital-based bereavement support groups encouraged people to understand that grief could last two years or longer. When Granger Westberg's classic guide *Good Grief* was first published in 1962, it described one of the effects of loss as "utter depression and desolation" and reminded readers that "such depression is normal and a part of good healthy grief."[18] Three decades later, bestselling behavioral science writer Daniel Goleman described the physical and emotional slowdowns of grief as helpful. Grief, he writes, "enforces a kind of reflective retreat from life's busy pursuits, and leaves us in a suspended state to mourn the loss, mull over its meaning, and, finally, make the psychological adjustments and new plans that will allow our lives to continue."[19] The *Diagnostic and Statistical Manual* through the 1994 *DSM-IV* recognized bereavement as a category separate from depression, allowing people space and time to walk slowly through their losses.

In the twenty-first-century United States, however, suffering deep sadness after a loss is no longer considered "ordinary functioning." Our accepted public ritual now involves up to three days of paid time off and up to two weeks of reduced productivity. The 2013 *DSM-5* reflects, and possibly helps promote, that cultural shift. According to *DSM-5*, if sadness extends beyond a two-week window, we might encourage a person to seek professional mental health care for the "clinical depression" that has resulted from the loss the person has suffered.

How can we go from having known for millennia that an extended period of sadness is the ordinary response to a significant loss to being convinced that a loss should be processed within a couple of weeks?

The answer might have something to do with the change in culture that would apply the word *process* to how we deal with a loss. "To process" has been used as a verb since the 1200s, beginning with uses that relate to lawsuits: what we still describe as the work of "process servers" and claim as our rights under "due process." The verb gained broader meaning as "a course or method of action" by the middle of the next century and found new meaning in nineteenth-century industrialization, "to subject to or treat by a special process." My 1991 edition of the *Oxford English Dictionary* has no citations for *process* that compare to our now common usage, "to process feelings." The closest it comes is a 1972 reference in neuroscience to the role of right- and left-brain hemispheres in "processing" oral symbols and verbs.[20]

"To process" an emotion makes addressing our feelings a technological activity within the human brain, analogous to what happens inside a computer's processors. Electrical impulses move down nerve cells and across synapses, conveyed by neurotransmitting chemicals and generating other emotional products. But if feelings are just the products of a process, it becomes first metaphorically possible, then clinically essential, to imagine Continuous Quality Improvement in our emotional outcomes. Our idea of "normal" mental health is upgraded. The twentieth century's "good grief" becomes the twenty-first century's "cheaper, faster, better" grief.

As we think of emotional processing as subject to the same efficiencies and improvements as industry, we move away from any traditional baseline of emotional norms. We accept a sliding scale of normalcy where the bar can be continuously raised, defining more and more people as having failed to meet the newly elevated standard of "normal."

Normal is a word that's remarkably hard to nail down. In medicine, it often describes various shades of ordinary: a normal lab result, normal blood pressure, a normal diet. Other times, medical professionals use *normal* and *the norm* as more aspirational terms. Doctors point patients toward norms that represent perfect health—not great health for a person your age or doing great considering what you're dealing with, but air-locked laboratory perfection.[21] In this framework, it is "normal" to be perfect. Or at least striving for perfection.

This way of defining the norm falls short when we try to transcribe it simultaneously across all the many arenas of our lives. In what part of my life will I be perfect? Will I target a perfect blood pressure, perfect weight, perfect relationship with children and spouse, perfect career trajectory, perfect image as a public Christian? What kind of perfection will I target? Pinterest perfect, résumé perfect, sanctification perfect? How many can I achieve at the same time? How many will I sacrifice to achieve others?

When it comes to mental health, raising the "normal" bar to perfection also creates problems when what we describe as perfect or normal for one may be abnormal or unhealthy for another. A height of seventy feet is perfect for a mature oak tree, unhealthy for a cornstalk, and terrifying for a spider. No one should try to attain the norm that God designed for someone else.

In fact, differing from the norm can be a gift to the community. Pediatric epidemiologist W. Thomas Boyce learned that some children's unusually sensitive responses to their surroundings could help signal environmental risks that might otherwise be overlooked. He labeled the more delicate young-sters "orchid" children, in contrast to the "dandelion" kids who thrive anywhere.

Boyce uses the old-time metaphor of the canary in the mine shaft to describe how these highly sensitive children experi-ence the world. Before electronic test equipment existed, coal miners used a caged canary to be sure a mine shaft was free from a dangerous buildup of toxic gases. As long as the bird sang, the miners were safe. If the bird stopped singing and fell over, gases had accumulated at a level hazardous to the canary but not yet toxic to the miners.

The bird's higher level of sensitivity protected the mining crew, even as it made the bird itself more vulnerable. The min-ers gained safety and security by allowing the bird to alert them to dangerous situations.[22]

Some of those we find challenging in our faith communi-ties are these "orchid" people. They are overwhelmed when a leader asserts demonic presence in their personal failings, confused when caught between varying versions of "truth." Sometimes, in difficult settings, they become explosive. They're not easy and they're not ordinary, but they also may not be mentally ill. Orchids aren't like dandelions.

SMALL BEGINNINGS: DISCERN WELL

When we define a medical norm aspirationally, then many people will fall short of the prescribed state of perfection. Likewise with our new, aspirational mental health norms. If half of us will experience the various kinds of suffering we call mental illness today, then facing most kinds of mental health problems is a normal life experience. Mental health professionals distinguish between the relatively rare "Serious Mental Illnesses" (creating severe impairment in about 5.2

percent of the US population) and the all-inclusive category of "Any Mental Illness" (one in five US adults in a recent year,[23] with one in two expected to suffer Any Mental Illness in their lifetime).[24]

When we extend the term *mental illness* to describe the lives of half the population, we are prone to become concerned about our own ordinary experiences. We also feel less capable of usefully helping troubled friends and neighbors. Many evidence-based practices for maintaining good mental health are probably already part of your life. You can be helpful by inviting a challenged friend to join you as you walk in a quiet park,[25] watch a funny movie,[26] or cook a healthy meal.[27]

THE CHALLENGE: NAMING A HEALTHIER NORMAL

Those of us who have lived in the United States during the last half century have enjoyed a way of life that offers levels of safety, comfort, and personal achievement unimaginable in most times and places. COVID-19 shattered expectations for many, leaving us in isolation, overwhelmed by new responsibilities, and unable to predict the future well enough to plan toward it.

Safety, comfort, and achievement can create their own illusion of mental health. We're calm because we are secure. We're happy because we are surrounded by enjoyable things. We're hopeful because we know, from personal experience, that the future will be better than the present.

The coronavirus pandemic overwhelmed those illusions as surely as a landslide overwhelms even a large building. We discovered that physical safety could be elusive and lost many comforts. We learned that our hopes were rooted in things that might not be so reliable: jobs, savings, schools, even the cleaning products on supermarket shelves. COVID most recently and the Great Recession not long before remind us that our normal lives in the United States have been exceptionally blessed.

But resetting our sense of normalcy is more difficult than resetting the thermostat when the season changes. We've come to believe not just that busy, cheerful, active lives are normal, but that we deserve them. We have become emotionally dependent on an exaggerated version of positive psychology: If you can imagine it, you can have it. If you can conceive it, you can achieve it.

Those upbeat attitudes carry a toxic corollary: when you fail, it's your own fault. And we think the same way about our mental health. We have created for ourselves expectations that go beyond anything God ever promised or imagined for us. We imagine we should be free from suffering, when God promised we would learn from suffering. We observe those around us in pain—or in unguarded moments, acknowledge our own pain—and expect an immediate remedy.

What have we learned from COVID? Some of us, not so much. We've learned that we're frustrated when we're not in control. Unhappy when we can't get what we want. Overwhelmed when we're responsible for maintaining all the parts of our very busy life: the house, the meals, the income, the kids, their education.

What might we learn from COVID? My great hope would be that as we return to our new normal, we carry with us new knowledge of how to live in challenging times. Because over the course of history, most times are challenging. And people do survive challenging times.

Difficulties can be the beginning of an unexpected and different life. But for people to recognize these opportunities, we need to stop naming normal mental health as what normal looks like only among the better-resourced members of an unusually wealthy and stable culture.

THE GOOD NEWS

The good news is that diagnostic and treatment fashions come and go. As incredible as it may seem that half of us will experience a diagnosable mental illness in our lifetime, there will come a day when this idea will actually *be* incredible. The more that God's people are willing to accurately name the challenges that people live with, the more readily we will recognize that a particular person is not suffering from the mental illness of "depression" but has been flattened by a huge boulder of life challenges. And when we see that boulder clearly, we may also recognize that we, as God's people, have the strength and the skills to lift the boulder and sit with the sufferer as she heals.

Many of those whose suffering seems greater than they can bear are not ill: they're orchids living in a time or community that has no use for their needs or their gifts. And many of those who readily thrive may benefit from observing in the orchids' suffering the early warnings of change that will eventually challenge them too.

We live together in Christ with people who are different from us and different from each other. God has meaning for the differences God created, and God has promised to work together for good even the differences that God neither created nor desired. Instead of being overwhelmed by the rising tide of diagnostic labels, we can trust God as we walk together—those diagnosed and those not diagnosed—in the life of Christ to which we are called.

2

How Culture Undermines
Mental Health

*I have never seen such loneliness as there is in the poverty
of affluence.*

—MOTHER TERESA

Many of us are accustomed to the idea that following God
might be a countercultural life journey. It's less familiar
to imagine that in the twenty-first-century West, good mental
health may also require some countercultural choices. In our
place and time, the demands and expectations of what we consider to be ordinary living can undermine mental health. To
keep our heads about us requires resisting the temptation to
follow those cultural trends and seeking a different way.

Even before pandemic-related isolation, loneliness had
reached epidemic proportions in the United States. That suggests a culture where many are isolated from any significant
sense of belonging. COVID-19 led to an upsurge in anxiety,

but anxiety—even by formal diagnoses—was already becoming an emotional norm. That suggests a culture where fear flows more freely than hope. As noted earlier, suicide and drug overdoses, together labeled "deaths of despair," consistently rank among the top ten causes of death in the United States.[1] That suggests a culture where hopelessness has overwhelmed so many as to make depression a common way of life.

Even as we recognize that loneliness and its cousins, depression and anxiety, have reached epidemic proportions in the United States, our highly individualistic culture can overlook structural causes in favor of individualized solutions.

No person's mental health problems belong to that person alone. Mental health issues have roots in genetics and family behavior patterns. They can be made worse by personal choices, including unhelpful behaviors and substance use. But mental health problems also are exacerbated by characteristics of cultures and communities. People who care about mental health—in others and in their own lives—must understand how their own culture influences mental health in order to guide themselves and others in healthy directions.

THREE AMERICAN EPIDEMICS: LONELINESS, ANXIETY, AND DEPRESSION

Several decades ago, executive Frank Butler and his wife, Ruth, took a pre-retirement trip to Kolkata, where they spent a week with Mother Teresa's Missionaries of Charity. The Butlers thought this could be the place to invest their next decades for maximum impact. Mother Teresa, Frank says, had a different idea.

"She put her hand on my knee and said, 'Frank, go back to America. In all my travels around the world, I have never seen such loneliness as there is in the poverty of affluence.'"[2]

A 2018 study by the Kaiser Family Foundation found that more than one in five US adults "always" or "sometimes" feels lonely or socially isolated.[3] US surgeon general Vivek Murthy published a bestselling book on loneliness, which grew in part from his observation as a practicing physician that "loneliness ran like a dark thread through many of the more obvious issues . . . like addiction, violence, anxiety, and depression" that plagued US culture.[4] Rates of expressed loneliness had doubled in the United States since the 1980s, he writes.[5]

Then came COVID-19, which physically separated us from at least some of the people who usually nurture and support us. While some were challenged by spending far more time than usual in close quarters with their closest relations, those who live alone lost even the once weekly round of handshakes at church or other community gatherings. It removed from many of us the daily sense of purpose we get in our jobs or schooling. It added new stresses from reduced income. It stripped from us the security of a relatively predictable future—even the security of a well-stocked supermarket. Those who did not suffer directly from the virus still suffered dramatic injuries to their sense of community belonging, as well as their certainty of meaningful contribution, life purpose, and future hope. At a moment when we faced remarkably large challenges, we were likely to be facing them without even ordinary social supports. We were alone. And lonely.

Even before the pandemic, as Americans expressed greater loneliness, we also became more likely to say we were anxious or depressed. The CDC believes that over our lifetime, half of us will experience these or another diagnosable mental illness—a remarkable statement about the mental health of a nation that has considered itself among the world's most blessed.

Loneliness, depression, and anxiety have been growing together because the same terrain nourishes them all. Loneliness is a sense of distress that comes when solitude is not welcome, and even before COVID-19 many of us were more alone than we wanted to be. Depression is a sense of distress that reflects, among other things, the loss of hope in a meaningful future. Anxiety has many causes, but one is the fear of facing large challenges without adequate help. In other words, one reason we feel anxious is because we too often face the challenges of life alone. One reason we feel depressed is because we too often believe the challenges we face alone will end in our defeat. And some people feel lonely simply because they are alone much too often.

WHY ARE WE SO LONELY?

Aloneness is, at this point, a cultural norm in the United States. In 2018, one-person households together accounted for 28 percent of all US households. Single women over age sixty make up a large portion—many widowed, some divorced, some never married.[6] The world has never before seen so many single-person households, and very few places in the world have even close to as many single-person households as we do.[7] Living alone doesn't automatically create loneliness, of course. Some people enjoy the quiet. Others, like me, live alone within the welcoming environment of a dense and very friendly neighborhood. At the same time, I find myself reflecting on how the prophet Isaiah described God's perspective on living alone: "Woe to you who add house to house and join field to field till no space is left and you live alone in the land" (Isaiah 5:8). God sees the isolated households of well-to-do communities as woe, not blessing. The percentage of us left to live by ourselves might be one symptom of the "poverty of affluence" that Mother Teresa described.

Younger people are also alone, although in different ways. They're less likely to live by themselves because their finances are more likely limited. They tend to stay busy because if they're not out, they're stuck in an apartment shared with near strangers. That happens in part because they're less likely to be married than youth of any previous generation.

Older adults may not readily recognize the aloneness felt by the young woman who is living through her fifth or sixth (or sixteenth) household transition since graduation. They can see that the mother of preschoolers feels alone in her hectic days of care, but are often less alert to the aloneness of the single man whose unmarried status isolates him from most church ministry except of that to other singles.

Loneliness is, predictably, associated with social isolation. We are not surprised to find older adults experiencing loneliness, since many live alone, often after the death of a life partner. Declining health may also limit their routine social interaction: a three-nation study found that 20 to 40 percent of those experiencing loneliness also have a disability or chronic illness.[8]

More surprising to many, loneliness affects younger adults more than older adults. Loneliness is especially likely to affect those with lower incomes, less education, and poor-quality housing. Why? Research doesn't have good answers, but the data does uncover something suggestive. People are more likely to feel lonely when they are dissatisfied with aspects of life that are common elements of how we find our fit with friends: finances, jobs, housing, and family life.[9] I think of one friend who almost never socializes at home, because she feels embarrassed to let the more successful members of her circle see that she lives in a mobile home. I find it difficult to socialize in circles where eating out is the standard, since frequent meals out challenge my budget. And almost every single adult has lost once-close friends to the closed club of married people.

Aloneness and loneliness are not just about the physical presence of others; they're about the quality of social connections we experience. But because we're a highly individualistic culture, we're prone to look for individual solutions to this social disorder. We offer cognitive therapies to help individuals overcome social anxiety. A lucky few may discover coaching systems that are good at teaching the skills of friendship. Some of the newest solutions include medicines to change the individual's biochemistry, since researchers find that people who say they are lonely also show biomarkers for inflammation and chronic pain.[10] Relieve the chronic pain, the thinking goes, and the associated chronic emotional tenderness may also be relieved enough to allow more consistent social interaction.

We experience loneliness as individuals. But to see it surging across an entire nation speaks to something larger than the individual failure of individual persons. It suggests that some viral infection of emotional discomfort has managed to spread among us—not a virus spread by contact, but a social disorder spread by non-contact, or inadequate contact, or (in some cases) inappropriate kinds of contact.

WHY ARE WE SO ANXIOUS AND DEPRESSED?
Anxiety is also on the upswing, according to many mental health statistics. Almost one in five US adults shows symptoms of an anxiety disorder, according to the Anxiety and Depression Association of America,[11] and a survey by the American

Psychiatric Association found that nearly 40 percent of adults were more anxious in 2018 than in the previous year.[12] That survey took place, notably, two years before the coronavirus pandemic.

The rise in youth anxiety has been particularly striking. The Higher Education Research Institute found that the proportion of first-year college students who reported feeling "overwhelmed by all I had to do" rose from 18 percent in 1985 to 41 percent in 2016. The American College Health Association found that 62 percent of undergraduates reported "overwhelming anxiety" in 2016, up from 50 percent in 2011.[13]

A wide range of current mental illness diagnoses include anxiety of some kind among their symptoms. The repetitive rituals of obsessive compulsive disorder—for example, always touching the fourth utility pole, checking the lock three times before leaving the house—are believed to be attempts to compensate for overwhelming anxiety. Many addictions begin with attempts to chemically alleviate uncomfortable feelings, including anxiety.

Increasingly, professionals view anxiety and depression as two faces of the same mental health problem. The Phobia Society of America refocused its work in 2012 as the Anxiety and Depression Association of America, in recognition that millions of people, including many of its members, experience both conditions.[14] Psychology professor Robert Kohlenberg says the evidence, over the last twenty years, shows that "the data are indicating they're not that distinct. . . . The diagnoses, particularly depression and anxiety, overlap."[15] For Allen Horwitz, a Rutgers sociologist who focuses on mental health issues, the shifting predominance of anxiety versus depression diagnoses over time just underlines the view that they are different names for essentially the same condition.[16]

OUR FEAR OF BEING (ONLY) HUMAN

Anxiety can be described as that pit-of-the-stomach feeling you get when you don't know what's next and whether you can handle it. It presages concern about just how hard the fall could be. It is often greater than the situation warrants, but that's part of its nature. Anxiety comes from parts of the brain that don't stop to think things through. It's rooted deep in body systems that are designed to get us away before a predator can attack us. It's part of the system God created to keep us safe from imminent harm.

Reliance on God alone is often presented as a simplistic solution to anxiety—as if an individual could swallow a "Fear not!" Scripture as readily as an antianxiety drug or a slug of booze. But this strategy often isolates the anxious person further. It can add a burden of guilt to the existing burden of fear. Has the person not tried hard enough to believe God's Word? Not remembered to repeat the Scripture verses often enough or loudly enough or consistently enough at the moments of need? Instead of drawing the individual deeper into the community of faith, it creates a new barrier to participation. "Fear not!" becomes not a welcome but a wall, something to be proved before full inclusion in the body of Christ is allowed.[17]

The paradox is that social safety systems—including God's own body, the church—are one of the ways that anxiety is often held in check. A teen may not know whether she can handle a gossipy classmate, but is confident her youth leader will help. An adult may be overwhelmed by hurricane damage to his home, but is reassured when a team from church shows up with tools and tarps. Sometimes, all we need is to know we're not facing our challenges alone.

Unfortunately, social systems can also add to anxiety. The role of social media in creating a sense of inadequacy is widely discussed. For me, seeing success (and parties! and vacations!) online isn't nearly as irritating as the chirpy exclamation of "Perfect!" that echoes through my days. Not that I think a cashier should chirp "Adequate!" when I fit my debit card into the reader. But if "perfect!" describes my ability to meet life's minimum daily requirements, what word describes me when I've accomplished something challenging? Or when I know without a doubt that I'm not "perfect!"?

The only way to be "perfect!" on a regular basis is to avoid doing anything I can't already do perfectly. Otherwise, I'm likely to fail. And the only way I can grant myself a "perfect!" when I've failed is to lie to myself. It's not really a failure; it's a "perfect!" first attempt. A "perfect!" bellyflop.

Those lies build a wall of deception around my real self. If my intent was a jackknife and I hit the water in a flat-belly splash, then to award myself the "perfect!" bellyflop medal is to deny meaning to my effort and purpose to my attempt. If I hold myself to "perfect!" as a standard, I force myself to choose among several unfortunate paths: self-limitation, self-deception, or failure. None of these offer any better than a fearful shortfall from the person God made me to be.

And if "perfect!" is a word I insist on using to describe myself, what word can describe my God? What distinguishes me from God?

Knowing that we are not God and fall far short of God's glory (Romans 3:23) doesn't stop us from striving to be perfect. Americans are an aspirational people. Contentment is not among our cultural virtues. The expectations we place on ourselves go beyond what many human bodies are made to handle. Young adults seek prescription and black-market stimulant drugs to meet the demands of schooling and professional jobs.[18] It is perhaps not surprising that a person attempting to live on four or five hours of sleep might require stimulants stronger than espresso and energy drinks. What is more surprising is that they—and we—accept such demands as a reasonable way of life for anyone. What kind of world have we created if we require performance-enhancing drugs simply to meet the expectations of daily life? And who are we, as individuals, if the only self we allow ourselves to be is a person enlivened by a drug?

Even short of this extreme, contemporary Western cultures are ruled by our ideas about effective use of time. "We value and desire efficiency, productivity, and speed, all of which derive from our conception of time," writes Daniel Rempel, a young scholar of disability and theology. "Why would we not want to do as much possible with the time we are given? The more we can do, the more *good* we can do. . . . The problem with equating goods like efficiency, productivity, and speed with Christian values is that it inherently relegates the role of a particular group of people in society. That group is people with disabilities."[19] We must equally add "those currently experiencing mental health problems," since at those moments, we also are generally not at peak performance. (The exception is, of course, those who are in a hypomanic swing. At these moments, our performance is often extraordinary, but our judgment frequently less so.)

And so we press anxiously forward, leaving behind those who can't keep up and—when we dare let the thought enter our minds—worrying about the day when we ourselves will likewise be left behind. That prospective loss lodges in our hearts as anticipatory grief. We become sad. Even depressed. We are less than we imagine, and therefore we imagine ourselves not enough.

THE "POVERTY OF AFFLUENCE" AFFECTS ALL OF US

How is it possible that we value ourselves so little when we live in a place and time filled with so much? The science carries us right back to Mother Teresa's concern about the poverty of our affluence. The social isolation and lack of stable, caring relationships that often characterize the well-to-do appear to have affected more than the top segment of our population—perhaps even most of our culture. Because our culture is wealthy.

The "poor little rich kid" has long been a staple of American fiction, and it turns out that fiction is not so far from fact. Children from affluent homes have emotional and social disorders that closely parallel those among kids who are impoverished. Psychology professor Suniya Luthar was surprised when the upper-middle-class control group in her study of low-income childhood dysfunction turned out to be "doing much more poorly" than the test group, "especially on drug and alcohol use and to some degree depression and anxiety as well."[20] Over subsequent years, she continued to find that affluent youth had high levels of substance use, anxiety, and depression, which she correlated with pressure to achieve and inadequate parental involvement.[21]

We've been ready to acknowledge that children in "at risk" families might experience mental health challenges. Seeing the same challenges in robust display among upper-income kids is startling. It also raises some questions about why we see these same challenges widely distributed across our population. Is it possible that we've unwittingly created an entire nation of "poor little rich kids" through a culture-wide pattern of affluence, stress, and isolation?

Global research on the prevalence of anxiety disorders supports the idea that anxiety rises not just with family income but with the typical level of income in a culture. A 2017 study of generalized anxiety disorder looked at the mental health of more than 147,000 adults in twenty-six countries. Researchers found that generalized anxiety disorder was more than three times as common in high-income countries (5.0 percent) as in low-income countries (1.6 percent).[22]

It hardly seems surprising that affluent kids experience mental health problems associated with isolation and stress. What may be more surprising is that the mental health problems associated with an affluent childhood also affect children and adults throughout our culture. Like other wealthy nations, we have reached a moment when most of us live what most of the world would see as "lifestyles of the rich and famous," complete with the associated mental health problems.

CULTURE CREATES OTHER MENTAL HEALTH PROBLEMS

COVID-19 has created an international laboratory demonstrating in a very large test group how sudden, radical change can create behaviors and thoughts that we are prone to call mental illness. Stripped of many routines and predictable elements of our days, burdened with new responsibilities to educate our children, hunt and gather toilet paper, make or obtain masks, protect public health, and maintain personal health, Americans flocked to hotlines with what we were told were symptoms of anxiety and depression.

And it was true: We were anxious. And sad.

But were these clinical conditions best remedied by counseling sessions and medications? Or were we confusing "mental illnesses" with the ordinary human response to unusual challenges—responses that would be unusual only if the circumstances were ordinary?

As a Jewish psychotherapist interned in German concentration camps, Viktor Frankl recognized that the abnormal conditions under which prisoners lived created responses that would be abnormal in ordinary life, but were appropriate to their environment. Survival required suppressing horror, disgust, and rage. A prisoner could watch unmoved as a doctor used tweezers to pluck off the gangrenous toes of a fellow inmate who had worked barefoot for many hours on frozen ground. Even years after release, a former inmate could respond in what seemed entirely inappropriate ways to images of camp-starved prisoners crowded onto sitting-room-only bunks. Frankl recalls seeing such a photo and thinking that the prisoners were fortunate: sick enough not to work but not so sick they were immediately killed.[23]

The pandemic forced many of us into behaviors that were unnatural for us and forced difficult feelings onto us. But even in the earliest months, some therapeutic professionals encouraged us to trust our ability to walk through difficult times without developing a diagnosable condition. Joshua Morganstein, chair of the American Psychiatric Association's Committee on the Psychiatric Dimensions of Disaster, told the *Washington Post* just days after the first lockdowns, "The vast majority of people, including all of us who are experiencing difficulties along the way, will ultimately do well."[24]

The mental illnesses we so feared during the coronavirus pandemic are likely to prove, by the time you're reading this, to have been mostly normal responses to abnormal circumstances. Is it possible that some part of the surge in diagnosed mental health problems over the last three decades also represents ordinary human reactions to attempting an abnormal way of life?

SHIFTING VALUES DESTABILIZE MENTAL HEALTH

Psychologist Jean Twenge studies how cultural changes affect our American way of life. In a study published in 2009, her team assessed data on college and high school students' mental health that had been gathered using the same test repeatedly between 1939 and 2009. Test results from over 63,000 college students and nearly 14,000 high schoolers showed that in the first decade of the twenty-first century, teens and young adults had significantly more symptoms of depression, paranoia, psychopathology, and hypomania than earlier generations did. The team concluded that the best explanation was "cultural shifts toward extrinsic goals, such as materialism and status and away from intrinsic goals, such as community, meaning in life, and affiliation."[25]

Twenge's outcomes are similar to the results of research worldwide, journalist Johann Hari notes. Studies done in the United States, Australia, Britain, Canada, Denmark, Germany, India, Romania, Russia, and South Korea can be summarized simply, he says: "The more materialistic and extrinsically motivated you become, the more depressed you will be. . . . the more anxious you will be."[26]

That is to say: The more we drive ourselves toward acquiring things, measuring our lives by things, and doing the kinds of activities that get us things, the more sad and fearful we become. We are assessing ourselves by measures that fall far below the measure of humanity God has instilled in us. And it is terrifying and sad to discover ourselves becoming unhuman. It barely matters whether we know ourselves to be followers of God and choose to measure our lives against what we understand of the Word. God has made all of us to live fully human in the image of God. When we fall short, some part of us knows that we have failed to be our own truest selves. We are sad we missed the mark and terrified we may never find our way to our own identity.

SMALL BEGINNINGS: THE PRAYERS OF THREE

Sometimes a simple act can have profound impact to push back the deep loneliness so many experience. One women's Bible study I attended began with prayer—not the pro forma gathering prayer we all know, but thirty minutes of prayer in small groups of three women. The groups were assigned at the first session and remained the same throughout the twelve-week study. Every week, each woman got ten minutes total to share her needs and receive prayer. The teacher called time to make sure each got her turn. The group's structure ensured we would practice two of the three cornerstones of friendship every week—consistency and vulnerability[27]—and it worked in our group to enfold three women whose childlessness might have left us marginalized within a family-focused congregation. When the study ended, our group of three was so closely bonded that we remain friends more than a quarter century later, despite life changes that have carried us across four continents.

THE CHALLENGE: MAKING A NEW WAY IN A STILL-OLD WORLD

In a culture that is shaped by affluence and its triple epidemics of loneliness, depression, and anxiety, how can your congregation be a place that nurtures connection, fearlessness, and joy? What can God's people offer a nation where any form of pain—physical or emotional—is quickly triaged to professional treatment in the hope it will be quarantined, if not cured? What hope can we offer people who are lonely and anxious, whether because of mental health problems or just because our culture today tends to create these forms of suffering? And do we have hope for those whose suffering is less common, who live with other kinds of mental health problems that we find even more challenging or fearful?

In the twenty-first-century United States, cultural expectations for growth and prominence can warp our expectations of how God should work in and among us. The culture has taught us to be dissatisfied with our own contributions if we're not among the "best"—even to feel humiliated by our limited measurable outcomes.

When we live as individuals under the tyrannical rule of these cultural expectations, we gather ourselves into churches where we are prone to tyrannize each other, simply because tyranny is the only way we know to relate. We find it hard to live graciously with each other's foibles because we've learned that your weakness could stand in my way. We find it hard to share—things, honor, opportunities—because we claim personal ownership of our achievements and our stuff. We live in individual and collective captivity to the anxiety, sadness, and loneliness that characterize our poverty of affluence instead of being rescued as a body into the wealth of God's gracious love.

THE GOOD NEWS: THE BROKEN ARE REBUILDERS

The good news for our culture, with all its manifold brokenness, is that God promises to use those who are devastated as rebuilders of the destroyed communities. For those of us who have been sidelined because of our brokenness, this is especially good news. In Isaiah 61, God offers "good news to the poor": the brokenhearted and mourners will be swaddled in God's comfort, the captives and prisoners will be freed. And these who are transformed from their suffering will be recognized as "oaks of righteousness, a planting of the LORD for the display of his splendor. *They* will rebuild the ancient ruins and restore the places long devastated; *they* will renew the ruined cities that have been devastated for generations" (Isaiah 61:1-4, my emphases).

Why? Why does God choose those who live with the greatest challenges to do the work of rebuilding?

Maybe it's because the ones who have lived with great suffering are the ones who understand how important it is to shape our communities such that no one will be forgotten or left behind. These are the parts of the body who know what a culture must provide for the sake of those who hurt. Theology professor Benjamin Conner notes that challenges, especially disabling challenges, can provide "a kind of hermeneutical advantage . . . for more fully understanding the human condition as people actually live it."[28]

And maybe God chooses the challenged to rebuild because we know that, however difficult or improbable our days, we still live in the constant presence of Father, Son, and Spirit. No matter how difficult my life or how difficult the other people I encounter, my life is lifted out of danger by the One-in-Three who threw out the lifeline to rescue me.

3

I Don't Feel Qualified to Help!

Human connection grounded in love and compassion always heals.

—**VIVEK MURTHY,** *Together*

Congregations are on the front lines where mental health problems are concerned. About one in four persons with a mental health challenge turns first to a faith community for assistance, and almost six in ten Protestant clergy report that they have counseled someone who was eventually diagnosed with a serious mental illness.[1]

At the same time, much of the mental health training available to people in congregations encourages us to step back from trying to help those with mental health problems. Most guidelines are designed only to help us recognize symptoms that make it advisable to refer people out to paid mental health professionals.

But how can it be possible that God's own body has no power to assist those who are suffering? We who are not counseling professionals still have important roles to play in the lives of those with mental health problems. There are many ways that ordinary Christians can provide good support and assistance to people who have mental health problems.

To the extent that mental health problems involve malfunctioning biological systems, most of us are unqualified to help. Where mental health problems carry persons into delusional worlds where we feel disoriented and uncomfortable, many of us need to step back and refer to a trained professional. But the care of people with mental health problems is, in most ways, very similar to the care of any person in the congregation. People with mental health problems seek help among the faithful for several reasons:

- We hope someone can convince us that our suffering has *meaning*.
- We want assurance that our difficult lives have *purpose*.
- We want to experience ourselves as persons who have *value*—persons who have been assigned an importance that often feels intangible by a God we cannot see, and who desperately crave recognition as valued individuals within the physically present body of Christ.
- We are looking for a place where we can *belong*, even when our mental health problems make us prickly and painful to be with.
- We are, with all the faithful, looking for "confidence in what we *hope* for and assurance about what we do not see" (Hebrews 11:1, my emphasis).

In helping us experience purpose, meaning, value, belonging, and hope, the pastor or fellow congregant functions not as a mental health professional but as a partner in faithful spiritual living. Caregivers don't need to have experienced mental health challenges to be present. We can listen. We don't need to know how to move a distressed person to a solution; we can simply sit with that person and seek understanding together with God. We can even be the experience of the ordinary that orients a sufferer to a place of safety in this world.

As one patient told a hospital chaplain, "You were normal, and right when I needed normal."

"I'M NOT A LICENSED PROFESSIONAL COUNSELOR"

Most training sessions for people in church leadership roles today include the reminder "You are not a professional counselor." This is a good and important thing: One friend, who teaches English to speakers of other languages at her church, discovered that a student was struggling in her marriage to a violent man. Because of her training, she knew to listen with kindness, find a helper skilled in mediating domestic abuse, and just remain available for side-by-side encouragement over the long haul.

Precautions against acting as a counselor can be a liability reminder. It's important not to claim expertise you don't have so you or your church can't be sued for failing to do something you were never qualified to do. It also helps pastors manage their limited time. A pastor friend says that standard seminary training for nearly three decades has been to provide no more than three sessions of pastoral care to any member of your congregation. After that, refer out to a professional.

Knowing our limits is generally a good thing. In the same way we would never assign a tone-deaf person to music ministry, it's good to keep people without empathy skills away from those who need grace-filled care. Those who are afraid of differences will be put off by those whose thoughts stray far from the ordinary. Even those of us called and gifted for care need to remember that we are responsible before God only for our care in fulfilling our task, not for the outcome in the person cared for.

For many of us, admitting limits is uncomfortable. We want to be helpful, we want to please the people around us, we want to appear competent in whatever situation we encounter. Yet there are real limits to the skills, time, and other resources most of us bring to our support of people with mental health problems. And it's very wise to acknowledge at least these limits:

- *We don't know enough to diagnose.* It's tempting to see a person who's struggling and hypothesize a diagnosis that would allow someone else to provide the care. It's one thing to say, "I think a specialist can bring some things to the table that we can't. Would you like to consider looking for a professional to help you through this?" It's a different matter to shut someone away from the normal avenues of congregational care when you believe the person could benefit from specialist help.

- *We don't know enough to prescribe.* This goes equally for licensed counselors who urge a particular medication and for lay counselors or friends who are excited about the medicine that worked well for someone they know. If we are not medical professionals functioning in our medical role, recommending specific medicines is dangerous.

- *We don't know enough to heal every emotional wound.* It's possible that God doesn't intend for this to happen in this life anyway. Jesus returned to earth with scars on his resurrected body so Thomas and everyone else would know that the glorified Messiah was the same person who had been spat on and hammered to a cross. Perhaps the emotional scars we bear are similarly part of our testimony to God's resurrecting power in our lives.

- *We may not be able to consistently and helpfully discern spirits.* Being labeled as demon-oppressed is an all too painful part of Christian life for many of us with mental health problems. I was fruitfully seeing a church-based counselor until he, with my permission, invited a congregational prayer leader to join us. She began praying that I'd be delivered from "the spirit of bipolar." I ceased to use that congregation's counseling center.

Many of us are cautious about bringing our mental health challenges to church because we know others who have been injured by bad church counseling. Dave's story from his childhood, some six decades ago, echoes too many that I've heard: "My sister was dangerous! She tried to hit my other sister over the head with a brick one day, and I told my mother, 'There's something wrong with her! She needs help!' And my mother told me, 'We just need to pray more.'"

Alice, meanwhile, didn't ask her parents to help a sibling. She wanted help herself. Even though she was a child, she was certain that the terror she experienced almost daily couldn't be normal. She knew classmates who took medicine. "Could I please go to a doctor?" she asked her parents.

Alice's parents said no. Followers of Jesus don't need medicine to escape fear, they said. They just need faith.

People like Dave and Alice leave church as soon as they leave the family home. What they've learned about God and the church is that no matter how well the church supports physical needs, there is no support when the challenges are emotional.

People like my friend Pete, on the other hand, have lived their faith for many years in congregations that allow them to receive help for mental health challenges without defining them by their mental health problems. Pete lives with schizophrenia and helped plant a church, was the pastor's prayer partner, was hospitalized more times than I know, and survived a suicide attempt that should have killed him. Pete is still friends with many people from his church. But even in this better scenario, a problem eventually emerged. Well-meaning congregants kept pushing Pete to give up the medicines that helped manage his mental health disorder and trust God alone for healing. (Ironically, no one urged him to trust God and give up his heart medicines.) Pete stopped attending church.

CHURCH CARE GOES BEYOND WHAT
PROFESSIONALS PROVIDE

The professional counselor and the medical professional can have important roles in the lives of many who live with mental health problems. But God has equipped the caring Christian friend and congregation for their own critical roles, even when professional care is available.

In a time when the care of mental illness is often referred out to psychiatrists and other medical professionals, it's worth remembering that very few mental health problems have exclusively biological causes. Our mental health is one of the most exquisite demonstrations of the intricate relationship that God created among our manifold selves as physical beings, social beings, thinking beings, and spiritual beings. Changes in any of these areas can affect any or all of the others. Weight loss offers a familiar example. We are more likely to make necessary changes in our physical routines—diet and exercise—when we make social connections with others who share those commitments. Revising our thinking about the size of a standard portion helps change our physical behaviors at meals and snack times. Some find motivation from a spiritual commitment to proper care of the body God has given. And the physical experience of a healthier, more energetic body can become a self-reinforcer for change.

Mental health practitioners often specialize in a particular form of care. So psychiatrists are far more likely to prescribe a medicine for depression than an exercise routine, even though the scientific evidence currently trends in favor of exercise.[2] Most psychiatrists are far more knowledgeable about managing medications than exercise management.

But you don't need to be a health professional to encourage your friend to go for a walk. Or to help her eat a healthy dinner. Most often, all you have to do is show up with your sneakers on or a nourishing meal in hand.[3]

Here are core areas where those without professional licenses can offer significant help to those living with mental health challenges.

Care for those in pain. Most congregations have various kinds of support for people in times of challenge—the meals brigade for new parents or those dealing with a hospitalization; the Stephen Ministry of lay chaplaincy for those in difficult circumstances. Psychology and neuroscience professor Matthew Stanford of Baylor University urges congregations to recognize three core responsibilities: to "relieve suffering, reveal Christ, and restore lives." These, he says, apply equally to those with physical or mental illnesses. He urges congregations to offer those with mental health challenges "a supportive care structure, help them spiritually, help them understand where God is in the situation, and help them connect more fully to God in their suffering."[4]

Help people find meaning and purpose. God says that each member of the body is essential to the body's functioning (1 Corinthians 12) and that God has set out responsibilities specifically designed for each member (Ephesians 2:10). Fulfilling the responsibilities God has given is part of how we experience meaning and purpose in this life. Priest and theologian Henri Nouwen writes, "Only those who truly believe they have something to offer can experience themselves as spiritually adult."[5] Conversely, congregations are able to do the work God has given them only as they allow members to do the work God has assigned to them. And congregants experience meaning when doing the work God has purposed for them.

Help people recognize the value God finds in them. The first chapter of Ephesians offers a remarkable picture of how valuable God considers us. In the prayer that opens the letter, the apostle Paul asks that the followers of Jesus would be given eyes to see "the riches of [God's] glorious inheritance in his holy people" (Ephesians 1:18). That is to say: We as people might look forward to inheriting money, a favorite piece of jewelry, even a family home. God "looks forward to" inheriting us. And God describes that inheritance as "riches" and "glorious." In other places, God names that inheritance as "a special treasure" or "my treasured possession" (Exodus 19:5 NKJV, NIV).

That's how much value God sees in us. God who created everything looks forward to claiming us. Even as we remind ourselves that we live as an "already and not yet" representation of God to the world, we ourselves are part of the "already and not yet" for God. We are already recorded in the book of life as part of God's inheritance, and we are not yet entirely in God's hands. And that is the value God intends us to see when we look at each other.

Help people experience belonging. Belonging is at the core of what it means to be a Christian. A Christian is a person who has been adopted into the family of God, becoming a child and heir of God (Galatians 4:5). Every Christian belongs, by definition, to a family that stretches around the globe and across centuries. But some Christians find it easier to experience belonging than others do. Belonging comes difficult to many with mental health problems, in part because of stigma. As congregations open themselves to value all the people God has brought to them, all the people God brings to them can experience in this world the belonging they already have in the body of Christ.

Congregations help people experience belonging by making sure they are not overlooked. Many revived their lay ministries of visitation during COVID-19 to make sure vulnerable individuals were not left in isolation. As appropriate, phone calls, virtual meetings, handwritten notes, and in-person visits have all been included. When well organized with clear guidelines, these visitation programs not only offer connections, but can afford opportunities for many who feel disconnected to become engaged in the work of connecting others.

Help people find hope. Hope happens when people discover a future they can believe will come. In the Bible, hope is a commitment, not just a feeling: it involves waiting for something (Psalms, Lamentations) and holding on to an expected future (Job, Jeremiah, Proverbs, and throughout the New Testament). People with mental health challenges often find it difficult to believe in a positive future. Our recent worldwide experiences of the Great Recession and the COVID-19 pandemic have made it easier for others to understand this lack of hope. Our uncertainties turned into our inability to predict tomorrow. And while people of faith know in our hearts that only God can see tomorrow, it's hard to walk forward with no idea about the destination. Our hopes are often rooted in the fulfillment of real-world promises—indeed, experiencing promises fulfilled is a core way we learn to experience hope.

Congregations and caring friends can help people dealing with mental health problems build hope by creating a predictable and reliable environment, keeping commitments, and walking alongside them on the often difficult roads to new habits, forgiveness, and relational restoration. Someone else's confidence in the path can give hope that the destination is attainable.

As nonprofessionals, we actually have some advantages in our mental health caring. Professionals who must focus on assessing people's symptoms can easily get stuck in measuring how close to or far from "normal" they are. A friend, on the other hand, can pay as much, if not more, attention to an individual's strengths. The Canadian Medical Association draws this point out in its tongue-in-cheek diagnostic review of A. A. Milne's Winnie-the-Pooh stories. Only Christopher Robin is okay, they found. Eeyore is clinically depressed; Pooh and Tigger have attention deficit hyperactivity disorder. Piglet suffers from a serious anxiety disorder, Owl has dyslexia, and Kanga has social anxiety.[6]

But the characters in the Hundred Acre Wood don't diagnose each other; they adapt to each other. In this, they benefit from several advantages from which we ourselves might learn:

- *They stay in one place and know each other over a long time.* Adaptation is more easily achieved when we allow ourselves time to do it. When we keep moving on in search of an easier set of friends, we don't learn how to live well with the friends God has brought into our lives. This is not, of course, a recommendation to adapt to a dangerous person. But it's often worthwhile to accommodate oddness and idiosyncrasy. Sometimes we even gain from it. What Eeyore doesn't need a bit of Tigger's enthusiasm from time to time?

- *They have limited options.* Milne's characters aren't free to pick up and move, or even to choose a new set of friends from a nearby field. Adaptation is more likely when it's clearly the best available option. In a culture that provides nearly endless options, it can be hard to believe that this difficult person is someone God has put in my life on purpose. Try to believe that God is really at work instead of rushing to find a new circle of aspirational friendships.

- *They know from experience that they'll do okay together.* Pooh will always be a "silly old bear" and Eeyore will always need more encouragement than others, but together they will do all right. And of course the calm, focused Christopher Robin helps keep the whole group together and moving forward.

The final advantage the characters enjoy is that they *are* fictional characters whose challenges are framed by the omniscient author as ordinary differences that can be overcome. We, on the other hand, sometimes forget that our challenges and our circumstances are equally in the hands of our omniscient Author. And perhaps our Author would also suggest that we live more nearly as if in the Hundred Acre Wood:

- *Know that this is the place and time God chooses for us.*

- *Value the people and opportunities that God has placed before us.*
- *Agree that muddling through together, in God's presence, is enough.*

Unlike our friends in the Hundred Acre Wood, we often lose track of the truth that most people with mental health challenges actually *do* manage. Our workplace relationships are too shallow; our neighborhood relations too transitory; our church behavior too proper. We undoubtedly know people with mental health problems, but we don't know them well enough to learn that these are more often challenges than catastrophes. So we lack a vision to be anything but seriously concerned should symptoms appear in our own lives or the lives of those we know well.

We also, perhaps, have lost the kind of good-humored tolerance that can welcome Eeyore despite his whining, and Tigger despite the danger he poses to the good china. Steve Macchia, who teaches spiritual formation for Christian leaders, suggests that "we've become judgmental; the twinkle in our eyes has been lost and replaced instead by a scowl and a frown. . . . Imagine if that were replaced with a wink of affection instead."[7]

Can you hear Christopher Robin now? "Silly old bear!"

Professionals have a role. So do nonprofessionals. And when I see what has been accomplished by nonprofessionals in other arenas, I wonder what opportunities we're missing when it comes to mental health.

In the 1980s, a mother angry that her thirteen-year-old had been killed by a drunk driver founded MADD, Mothers Against Drunk Driving. The members of MADD weren't experts in the chemistry of alcohol addiction or the science of treatment. They just wanted to keep their children safe. And in less than two decades, they sparked a public movement that dramatically cut the rate of alcohol-related traffic deaths in the United States. Measured against vehicle miles driven, the alcohol-related traffic death rate per mile driven dropped 62 percent. Almost equally important, the rate of traffic deaths not related to alcohol also dropped by 19 percent.[8] By creating an environment where it became less acceptable and less possible to kill people by driving drunk, MADD and its partners also created an environment where it was less possible to die in any auto accident.

The biological science of addiction has taught us a lot that helps people more successfully survive their tendencies to addiction, but so too did a group of fierce women who chose to focus on harnessing the power of their communities.

SMALL BEGINNINGS: LEVERAGE EXISTING STRENGTHS

As mental health nonprofessionals, we can be both caregivers and changemakers. Referring to professionals is fine, but it's also fine to power up the gifts God has given us to offer support in tandem that only the church can provide. The hospitable: by inviting and welcoming. The lighthearted: by including and attuning to laughter. The patient: by sitting with and listening. The prayerful: by sitting with and lifting up. Our God-given ability to support others entirely outside the boundaries of professional disciplines could become our greatest nonprofessional strength in supporting people with mental health challenges.

THE CHALLENGE

As nonprofessionals who care for people with mental health problems, we face a great many challenges. How will we respond when we can't make sense of someone else's confused words? How do we encourage when a person's ambitions seem like unrealistic fantasies? How do we sustain hope—in another and in ourselves—when yet another medication change has yielded no helpful result?

All of these are difficult. Still, the largest challenge we experience as nonprofessionals who care for people with mental health problems is accepting that we aren't, ultimately, in control of the outcomes. Professionals face the same challenge, of course, but their professional training and peer supports help them place a bright line between their own considered "best practice" treatments and outcomes that are not fully under their control. For nonprofessionals, it's a little different. Suicide in particular can threaten to drag us along in an undertow of recriminations and guilt.

As nonprofessionals, we face limitations in what we bring to our mental health caregiving. We must allow individuals to seek medical and diagnostic care, and we must avoid offering diagnostic labels we're not qualified to name. We need to avoid what has become a culture-wide willingness to label ordinary conditions with diagnostic words. "Depressed" isn't what we feel when our sports team falls behind. Clinical "anxiety" isn't the same thing as being worried about how the coronavirus is affecting our loved ones and employees. "Can't sit still!" isn't usually ADHD, and maintaining carefully organized rows upon rows of coins in page after page of albums is almost never a symptom of obsessive compulsive disorder.

Accepting limits is hard for many of us. Living within limits is difficult in an aspirational culture like the United States. Moving forward with our friends who are currently limited by their mental health problems, knowing that at any moment we may bang up against our own limited knowledge, limited skill, and limited compassion, is frightening and humbling.

THE GOOD NEWS

The good news for nonprofessionals who care about people with mental health problems is that we are not responsible for diagnosing and fixing their condition. God may heal or not. God may lead the person to a medical treatment that works or not. God may lead the person to a counselor who is wise or not. And depending on our own level of knowledge and community connections, we may get to be part of God's referral system that sends the individual to these kinds of good help.

The part every one of us is responsible for, as Christians, is to represent God to that person who is experiencing mental health problems. We're responsible for enacting the kinds of care that God has empowered us to provide that person.

Often, that care is as ordinary as daily human encouragement toward healthy activity. One of the things that make me happiest about our growing mental health evidence base is that so much science reinforces what humans have known for centuries. Rural schoolteachers of my grandmother's era knew that fidgety kids needed to get moving, whether to run around outdoors or to bring in heavy armloads of wood for the classroom stove. Today, we prescribe "motor breaks" of physical activity. Angry kids back in the day were urged to take a deep breath and count to ten before they spoke hurtfully, just as professional counselors remind us today. Parents pushed children outdoors for fresh air activity—what we now might call "nature bathing"—for hours every day.

Mental health professionals are sometimes helping us come back around to solutions known for generations. So we discover again (as did Martin Luther and William Cowper in their own times) that being alone is not helpful—that going any place where we'll encounter people is smart, but failing that, pets or farm animals are better company than our own overactive and unhappy minds. We discover activities that, by their intellectual or physical rigor or both, can fill enough mental channels to push out, at least for a time, the problems that otherwise occupy those spaces. Keeping busy is its own kind of remedy. Luther said, "The human heart is like a mill-stone in a mill: . . . if you put no wheat [under it], it still grinds on, but then 'tis itself it grinds and wears away."[9] Or as our grandmothers might have put it, more simply, "Idle hands are the devil's playground."

Most congregations have no end of things that need doing. These activities can become part of a person's mental health treatment when those tasks make us part of a team, allow the team to benefit from the real gifts and skills we have, and—this is the rub—can be handed off or postponed when we are simply not able to do them. Because sometimes that will happen.

For me, my volunteer healthcare chaplaincy has been among the best of these. It uses my exceptional ability to hear behind a person's words and understand what's really happening. It relies on my willingness to sit with uncertainty when I don't understand. It adds a block of scheduled time to weekends that—for a single person like me—can flow very long and empty. It puts me among a familiar group of assisted living staff and residents every Saturday. And during autumn months, when my annual emotional cycle means I am most likely to be challenged to the point of incompetence, I can just skip a shift. I'm a volunteer. Having been present for most of the weekends of the year for two years makes me a valued teammate. The five or six I miss each year to depression pale in comparison.

Each of us lives with our own emotional challenges, and in reality those may make us better caregivers. The caregiver who expresses an emotion in harmony with what the cared-for feels is doing something that professional counselors are generally forbidden: showing that the caregiver has brought his or her own heart into the counsel. At that moment, the caregiver is not just teaching or modeling or proclaiming a new approach to difficulties, but entering the world of the person cared for and inviting that person into the caregiver's own way of handling challenges.

The counseling profession, by its current standards, requires both counselor and counselee to walk a highly unnatural emotional tightrope. On one hand, the success of the therapy requires the counselor to establish emotional rapport with the client. Yet the profession defines the counselor as being so emotionally distant from the client that should the two meet in public, the counselor would pretend to not know the client out of concern for the patient's privacy.

The congregational caregiver holds confidences, but cannot hold such a distance. We walk humbly beside the person in need, acknowledging that we, too, are often in need. The good news for all of us who care and need care is that our God is big enough to care for all of us. And our God cares for us through the manifold gifts provided to each of us in the body of Christ and in the world God created and owns.

Thanks be to God.

4

Discovering Meaning and Purpose

To ask "What is the meaning of life?" is like asking a chess grandmaster "What is the best move?". . . Everyone's task is as unique as is his specific opportunity to implement it.

—**VIKTOR FRANKL**, *Man's Search for Meaning*

It all came to a head for me one chilly October afternoon. Who knows why one day is more desperate than another. All I know is that as I pulled into my parking spot after work, I wasn't just promising myself I could die. I was ready.

I knew that the moment I opened the front door, my house-mates' three children would wrap themselves around me in the warm welcome I always enjoyed. But I couldn't bring myself to stir from my car. At that moment, I heard a familiar voice speak—the Voice I know as God.

"Plant bulbs," it said.

"Huh?" I thought. I mean, talk about a non sequitur. I'm sitting in my VW Beetle ready to die, and God is telling me to plant bulbs? Seriously?

"If you don't have a reason to live till spring, plant bulbs," God answered.

Oh.

As soon as I stepped across the threshold, the kids hurled themselves at me, and I could smell dinner almost ready. When we all sat down at the huge dining room table, I asked my housemates if they'd consider chipping in to buy spring bulbs for the yard.

A few days later, with dozens of crocus, daffodil, hyacinth, and tulip bulbs in a clutter of small paper bags around me, I began to dig. By the end of the month, the bulbs were tucked in for the winter and my death wish was temporarily at bay.

I'd love to say that I was free of suicide impulses from that day forward, but that wouldn't be true. I continued to console myself at the end of bad days—which were most days—with the promise I could die anytime I wanted to. The count hit more than seven thousand days by my best estimate. I continued to stay alive by planting both garden bulbs and the metaphorical bulbs of kind deeds, and also by remembering that God cared enough about me to tell me directly what to do.

WHY?

It's the most fundamental of questions. It's the one we bring to our pastors and friends after a loved one dies. It's the one children use endlessly in their attempt to make sense of God's world.

Why is the sky blue? Why do cats purr? Why do acorns make trees?

The questions grow more difficult as we live longer. Why was my spouse among the ones laid off? Why did my mother have to die alone during COVID? And while we often don't understand God's meaning in this world, we often do understand how to *be* God's meaning in this world.

Be kind.

Do to others as you wish they'd do to you.

Do the right thing.

Show up.

Why?

Because the right thing matters to God. And God matters to us, and we matter to God.

Gerda Weissmann Klein, a survivor of World War II concentration camps, told a poignant story of an imprisoned child who still managed to live in accord with her sense of meaning. In that terrifying, sparse place, the girl found a plant with a single ripe red raspberry.

To a starving person, food is food. I can imagine scarfing down the one berry in an instant, then ravaging the surrounding area in the desperate hope of finding any others.

Not this child. This starving girl, Ilse, carefully plucked the berry and carried it in her pocket all day. That evening, she presented the single berry as a gift to her equally starving friend Gerda.

As Klein reflected: "You can imagine a world in which your entire possession is one raspberry, and you give it to a friend."[1]

Part of what it means to be human is to shape our living by what gives meaning to our lives. That's why providing for our family is sufficient grounds to keep so many working for years in jobs we don't love. The meaning isn't the job but the family.

We find it difficult to live when meaning has been torn from our lives. That's one reason grief holds us in its grip so long. When we lose a person who was important to us, we flounder amid days emptied of our loved one's presence and the habitual interactions that fed our daily sense of purpose. We need to find new ways to experience purpose without that person.

Psychotherapist Viktor Frankl honed his therapeutic model as an inmate in German concentration camps during World War II. To inmates ready to die "because they had nothing more to expect from life," Frankl issued a challenge. He urged them to discover what life was still expecting from them:

"Life ultimately means taking the responsibility to find the right answers to its problems and to fulfill the tasks which it constantly sets for each individual," Frankl writes. "Life's tasks are very real and concrete. They form man's destiny, which is different and unique for each individual."[2]

What matters, Frankl says, is not what we expect from life but what life expects from us. We might rephrase: it doesn't matter what we expect from life. Life is a gift from God. What matters is whether we receive the gift with gratitude and live to demonstrate the value we place on both the life and its Giver. The tasks God has assigned to each of us are those that are before us. Responding to them, whether well or poorly, is how we reflect our willingness to follow God into the purpose God has set for us.

Lutheran pastor Brad Hoefs was following his purpose as pastor to a growing congregation when a bipolar mania derailed his work and discredited his ministry. He remembers the 1995 congregational meeting when a staff colleague described him as having failed to "finish well." And he remembers thinking, *Finish? I'm thirty-seven years old. This isn't the finish.*[3] Hoefs lost his pastorate. What would be next?

Happily for Hoefs, a group of supportive Christian friends stood by him through a long period of recovery. Over ensuing years, Hoefs became certified as a peer support specialist to others with mental health problems. Peer support specialists are those who are particularly well equipped to assist people with mental health problems because they have lived with those challenges themselves. Their work is grounded in the recovery model of mental health care and directly demonstrates that model's effectiveness. Hoefs eventually returned to the pastorate and founded a powerful peer-driven mental health ministry, Fresh Hope: a place where people are regularly reminded to identify sources of hope to continue overcoming their challenges.

During our long and sometimes tortuous human journey toward our ultimate hope, faith communities can promote better mental health among *all* members when they intentionally seek and embody beliefs that echo the recovery model:

- *Value*—Our faith teaches us that our life in this world matters. Each individual life matters. Each person is a unique being who brings unique value to this world.
- *Meaning*—Because each life has value, each life is interwoven into the overarching meaning that God intends for this world.
- *Purpose*—What each person does matters. Each person has been created and shaped to accomplish something—small or large, publicly visible or not—that advances God's work.
- *Belonging*—God holds us as if we are carved into God's own hands and knits us into the living body of believers. Our belonging among God's people is entirely indissoluble.

- *Hope*—Even when suffering seems likely to persist in this life, the people of God know there is a time ahead when all our tears—even the salt that flavors them—will be gone.

I find much of the truth of the mental health recovery model in a short Scripture passage, Ephesians 2:8-10. Here, God tells us: "For it is by grace you have been saved, through faith—and this is not from yourselves, it is the gift of God—not by works, so that no one can boast. For we are God's handiwork, created in Christ Jesus to do good works, which God prepared in advance for us to do."

This text speaks directly to our meaning and purpose, reminding the Christian that we have been re-created as God's own handiwork, designed to "do good works, which God prepared in advance." It says that God has not only made us competent for what God wants done, but laid out those good works ready for us to accomplish.

The passage also speaks powerfully of our value. It describes us as God's own handiwork. The original language is even stronger. It calls us God's *poesie*, a word that is used for any created work but also refers specifically to poetry. We are, each one of us, an original work of poetry spoken into existence by the One Word who spoke into being all words, all beings, all that is and will be. As lyrical words spoken into being by the Word, we have profound value and unmistakable meaning for God's kingdom.

As each of us finds a place of belonging among God's people and in God's world, we find our opportunity to live out the value, meaning, and purpose God has designed into us. And those opportunities have been laid out in advance by God for us: we can live forward in hope of discovering and accomplishing them.

So many tasks assigned by God must be accomplished in this world and no other:

This is the only world in which I can comfort a person who is in grief.

This is the only world in which I can feed a person who is hungry.

This is the only world in which I can visit a prisoner.

This is the only world in which I can, by God's power, drive out demons.

This is the only world in which I can offer a job to a person who is in need.

This is the only world in which I can welcome a stranger—whether that's an immigrant, someone I don't know yet, or someone who is even stranger than me.

It's a hard truth that relieving others in their suffering doesn't relieve us of that pestering "Why?" We still wonder why a certain individual suffers in a certain way. We rarely find the full answer we crave. Instead, we find some part of our own meaning and purpose in the work God has given us to help another. We don't understand why others suffer. But we do discover part of why God has placed us in their lives. By God's kindness, we are to be friends. We will meet some of their needs today, and by God's grace, they will meet some of our needs tomorrow.

WHY DOES SUFFERING MATTER?

British prime minister Winston Churchill suffered from depressions so dark that under their influence, he avoided the edges of subway platforms for fear he would throw himself in front of trains. He described his depression as a "black dog" that hounded his steps, drawing on an image from the Roman poet Horace. The black dog was an unhappily faithful companion.

Still, it was not part of him. There was Winston and there was the depression. There was the politician, and there were the mental health problems.

We tend to view depression differently in the twenty-first-century West. Today, we describe it as part of oneself, at the molecular level. And today, we not only assume it possible to fight despair, but generally presume anyone responsible to do so. Quickly. With professional mental health care.

Our twenty-first-century depressions are, unfortunately, not always more consistently remedied by the medical treatments now available than were the depressions of past centuries. Researchers don't even agree that antidepressant medicines work better than inactive placebo drugs.[4] But because we believe that mental health challenges should be quickly fixed, we often find them harder to live with. The unhappiness caused by the suffering itself "is increased by unhappiness about being unhappy," twentieth-century psychologist Edith Weisskopf-Jo-elson observed. The sufferer "is not only unhappy, but also ashamed of being unhappy."[5]

And yet depressions, like most kinds of suffering, serve a purpose. Suffering signals that something is wrong. Some of the issues that cause suffering can be remedied individually: a sin that needs repenting, an expectation out of whack with circumstances, a bad habit that leaves a body cranky and ill-tempered. Perhaps the problem is in the person's biochemistry, as many current mental health treatments emphasize. Suffering often signals loss, whether a recent loss or one not adequately grieved. Maybe an individual was traumatized by some experience and has not found a way to resolve it.

But even though some suffering is related to individual concerns, suffering can also mean that we're missing something in our common life. This is obvious when some suffer from lack of such essentials as food or shelter. As social beings, we may also suffer from isolation and social exclusion. We suffer when we experience social losses: the loss of people we love, jobs we enjoy, community connections that we value. As we struggled to contain the coronavirus through social distancing, we saw the pains of loneliness, fear, and sorrow spread across the culture. It seemed evident that these mental health problems resulted from challenges our entire communities were facing, not any individual causes.

Most broadly, suffering occurs because of sin. We suffer because we sin. We suffer because someone sins against us. We suffer under the oppression of culturally accepted sins. We suffer because the world we live in has been marred by past sin and current sin. Our world is not as God intended it, and we suffer for it.

Suffering matters because it is the most profound proof we can find that we were not made for this world as it currently exists. It demonstrates to our hearts that the world in which we live has been fundamentally spoiled. It gives evidence that this world is no longer as God created and intended it. And as such, suffering is our most powerful pointer toward the world that will one day be as God intends it to be.

Unobserved suffering also matters. When we turn away from suffering that we see, we are warned that our hearts have turned from the compassion God intends. When we turn away from only certain kinds of suffering, that signals how highly we value the opposite blessing. When we fail entirely to see some kinds of suffering, that tells us where we have become spiritually blind—sometimes as individuals, but often as a culture.

Spiritual blindness is baked into the very structure of twenty-first-century US communities. We build neighborhoods without sidewalks or crosswalks because we are blind to those without cars. We construct what we call "moderate income" housing that is affordable only on two full-time incomes because we are blind to the huge population of single adult and low-wage households. We applaud ourselves for transitioning people with mental illnesses out of institutional care, and then fail to see that our prisons have become the new, de facto mental health hospital system.[6]

Spiritual blindness to the suffering of others often points to our own most cherished idols. We overlook those without cars, spouses, and full-time jobs because we imagine these fundamental to mature adulthood. We overlook those whose lives are still marked by our national legacy of racism because we imagine our own lives free of its benefits. We fail to care for those imprisoned with serious mental health problems just as we fail to care for all who are imprisoned because we are confident they must deserve their pain just as we deserve our better circumstances.

SUFFERING CAUSED BY MORAL INJURY

A growing discipline in therapeutic care recognizes that certain kinds of suffering are rooted in damage to the moral identities we carry at the core of our human life. The field of moral injury has grown from the treatment of military personnel returning from combat in the late twentieth and early twenty-first centuries. These soldiers had familiar symptoms of post-traumatic stress disorder (PTSD)—flashbacks, bad dreams, frightening thoughts; excessive levels of anxiety, sadness, or anger; exaggerated startle reactions; physical symptoms like sweats, high blood pressure, racing hearts.[7] But something else was also going on.

What professionals recognized was that the terrorist strategies that changed the nature of warfare also challenged some core beliefs and practices of our military. US military life has historically held to a certain set of moral values. You don't kill noncombatants. You don't leave a comrade behind. But modern warfare was forcing in-the-field decisions to abandon those values. A unit might be ordered to kill an approaching woman or child out of concern that they were carrying explosives. Soldiers could be ordered to leave an injured comrade behind because in that combat theater, fallen soldiers had been used as bait to draw the rest of their unit into sniper gunsights.

Actions like these were tearing at the hearts of many military men and women. They considered themselves moral actors in a world where right and wrong matter. Being ordered (or required by the situation) to take actions that violated their sense of right and wrong damaged them at the center of their own moral belief and damaged their ability to believe in trustworthy moral authorities.

The new diagnosis of moral injury describes a specific kind of PTSD that includes these kinds of damage to moral belief and moral identity. People who have experienced moral injury can lose trust in moral authorities and also in their own power to take actions that are in tune with their most deeply held moral convictions.

Although moral injury has been named in veterans' care, it is easy to see how it might be recognized in civilian life. Sexual abuse is an obvious example. Adults who lived with sexual abuse during childhood were betrayed by a moral authority and forced to violate their own God-made moral compass. As the #ChurchToo movement has gained strength, we have recognized that this violation of moral trust even by church leadership is more common than we have ever wanted to acknowledge. Sexual harassment and abuse of adults also inflicts moral harm, and the global #MeToo movement testifies to its broad impact.

A different kind of moral injury occurs when the marginalization of certain groups becomes foundational to a culture. In 2020, the built-in racism of American culture became particularly visible in casual police brutality like that which killed George Floyd. It was visible in the kind of discriminatory policing practices that placed riot shields and tear gas between protesting Black Americans and the Capitol, whereas White insurrectionists were allowed to parade the flag of secession through our national legislature. Smartphones make it possible to share these murders and injustices in real time, making all of us witnesses or complicit bystanders and potentially subjects of moral injury

The Shay Moral Injury Center at the Volunteers of America extends the definition of moral injury to reach almost everyone. They define moral injury as "an affliction of conscience, identity, and meaning because of harm we cause, witness, or experience from others" and recognizes that anyone "with a working conscience" who violates their own moral code may experience moral injury.[8] The center offers training for clergy, chaplains, and mental health professionals, among others, in this new discipline.

Trauma-informed therapies are generally the closest civilian equivalent to what the military is accomplishing in the field of moral injury. Trauma-informed therapies recognize that something happened to a person that has undermined that person's sense of identity, security, and competence. The injury may be a single incident or may involve long-term exposure to social factors such as poverty or racism. The Sanctuary Institute describes trauma as "an experience in which a person's internal resources are not adequate to cope with external stressors," making it clear a specific circumstance can affect different individuals very differently.[9] These injuries can cause long-lasting damage to an individual's physical and emotional health, social relations, thought processes, and spirituality.[10] The Trauma Healing Institute explains trauma in simplified language: "Trauma is a wound of the heart and mind that causes deep suffering. It leaves us feeling overwhelmed and disconnected. It takes a very long time to heal. It hurts every part of us."[11]

Physical trauma is easy to conceive. It's easy to recognize trauma in the person whose home has been overwhelmed by floodwaters. Some kinds of emotional trauma also seem obvious. I think about the grade-schooler I knew who tried to casually toss off the impact of seeing a neighbor shot to death on the street. "It wasn't in front of my house," she said.

But more specifically moral traumas also exist in our civilian culture. A college student who realizes his parent bribed admissions officers loses his identity as a successful student and his certainty in taught values of hard work and integrity. Healthcare providers during the coronavirus pandemic experienced moral conflicts as they kept dying patients isolated from their families. An adult child making end-of-life decisions for an unconscious parent may feel she is making choices that "no one should make" between allowing her mother to suffer or allowing a higher morphine dose that will hasten death. The responsibility to provide loving care collides with the responsibility to preserve life, creating a no-win moral trauma.

This is the stuff of moral injury, but most civilian counseling models attempt to function without reference to moral systems. With the exception of legal settings, the word *shame* has tended to replace *guilt* in recent years, and that's unfortunate. Treating guilt with the social acceptance that alleviates shame will not reduce the pain of guilt. Sloughing off guilt as if real violations of God's moral code require any less than confession, repentance, and restitution creates a toxic moral environment, and toxic moral environments undermine mental health for all. God built a moral core into all of us, and trying to overlook it creates mental health problems. We're simply not built to tolerate that.[12]

WHY DOES MENTAL HEALTH SUFFERING MATTER?

The suffering we experience because of mental health problems poses a specific set of challenges, as it often has no clear cause or relief. If we could easily find the reason, we could easily establish the meaning. And of course, that's how many prefer to minister. Like Job's comforters, they look for unrepented sin and accuse the suffering one of bringing pain onto themselves. They can drive those already afflicted into an agony of self-examination and self-accusation, appearing to have forgotten that "all have sinned and fall short of the glory of God" (Romans 3:23). They do not remember that those who live without mental health problems, just like those who are tormented by them, are also people who have failed to live according to God's glorious purpose. When we accuse those in emotional pain of being to blame for their pain, we claim our own emotional stability as a sign of God's blessing on our good habits and life choices, instead of a simple sign of God's unmerited blessing.

And then what happens when we experience our own seasons of pain?

The mental health challenges so many have experienced in response to COVID-19 remind us that suffering is likely to come to us all. The pandemic's generous distribution of emotional difficulties may help us remember in the long term that, in the words of author and professor Rosaria Butterfield, "God's distribution of crosses is not democratic. I may get one cross, and you may get ten. The job of an ally is to accompany someone in her suffering and to carry some of the load of cross bearing."[13]

SMALL BEGINNINGS: UNCOVER MEANING AND PURPOSE

When people who are suffering cannot find meaning in their difficult lives, we must believe on their behalf that meaning exists. When they cannot see purpose, we must be confident that purpose is set.

Most of us are not given to see the meaning or purpose in another's life. Our efforts to make meaning for others often pop out in jarring phrases that feel like disparaging cliches. "It's all part of God's plan." "God works in mysterious ways." "I wonder what good God is accomplishing through this."

But as we sit quietly with people who are suffering, our very presence can remind them of God's presence with them. We ourselves can hold confidently to the truth God has given: even this challenged person is God's own *poesie*, created in Christ Jesus to do good works, which God has prepared in advance. We can remind suffering people that meaning and purpose exist for their life and can hold them close as they seek to discover for themselves the meaning God sees in them and the purpose God has given to even the very difficult moment they face.

THE CHALLENGE

Will we partner in God's work of creating meaning or be sucked into the destructive work of despair?

Anglican priest Katheryn Greene-McCreight, who lives with bipolar disorder, describes the despair that accompanies so many mental health problems as nothing more than "evil . . . a black hole, a void, an emptiness that sucks into itself the sufferer." Yet she reminds us, "God is the One who called order out of chaos . . . and God calls even us into creation out of nothingness into life before him."[14]

God assures us that every part of the body is needed. "To each one the manifestation of the Spirit is given for the common good" (1 Corinthians 12:7), God tells us. Those blessings on behalf of the entire body are given not just to those with large social media followings, big homes for entertaining, or prominent community roles, but to each one who belongs to God. Beyond that, God even asserts that the pain of any member injures all the members. "If one part suffers, every part suffers with it" (1 Corinthians 12:26).

THE GOOD NEWS

Before the coronavirus pandemic, we liked to believe we were all doing fine and we all knew where we were going. We weren't so fine that we could all live without mental health medicines: in fact, we weren't fine enough to be sure most of us would get through life without a diagnosable mental illness. We weren't so sure of our direction that we could always name it. Maybe our direction was just somewhere better: a faster speed in the 5K, a higher-paying job, a bigger following on social media, a better education for our children.

Then the coronavirus struck down almost all the paths we knew to follow. What purpose did we have without access to our goals? What meaning could there be in a life constrained to four walls and a Zoom screen?

Some of us rallied to new goals. Cartoonist Stephan Pastis depicts "Steady Susan," who says she has made "great use of my time during COVID" to exercise, organize her home, read, and spend time with her kids. "So I'm better read, more fit, more organized, and a better parent," she asserts with a broad smile.

And then she loses it. She screams, "I want my life back!"[15]

That's the rub, isn't it? When we're afforded the chance—or forced by circumstance—to try a different approach to life, we can recognize our new kinds of accomplishments, but it's still hard to let go of the life we imagined would be ours.

Those of us who live with serious mental health problems have often already learned to relinquish much of our sense of life as we could have imagined it. We sometimes struggle to find meaning and purpose within the constraints we experience.

And yet people with mental health problems must seek and find meaning and purpose within the limitations of our invisibly walled lives. As people of faith, we all remember that God has given us only the specific day, place, body, and challenges that are before us now. In this very spot, living with the constraints we currently endure, will we find the "good works, which God prepared in advance for us to do" (Ephesians 2:10). And as we walk into these, we experience the meaning and purpose God provides.

5

Belonging: Where Stigma Ends

It's when we are least lovable that we most need each other's love.

—**DOROTHY LITTELL GRECO**, *What's Faith Got to Do With It?*

Isolation is emotionally challenging. There's a reason it's one of the stress techniques used to pressure information out of prisoners of war. Isolation can crack the average person's ability to remember who they are and what matters most, stripping them of identity and purpose. And COVID left many of us far more isolated than usual, causing some of us to experience what may have been our first extended periods of being alone.

Mental health problems also tend to isolate people. Many of us, including those with mental health diagnoses, are more likely to draw inward than reach out in our most difficult moments. Stanley Hauerwas writes, "The dangerous thing about mental illness is how it tempts those so afflicted to think they are completely on their own, isolated in their distress."[1]

But we are also likely to be, in fact, more alone than many others. People with mental health problems have fewer friends. We are more likely to count our family members as friends. We are less likely to have untroubled people in our friendship networks: most of our friends are also people with mental health problems.[2]

Some see our social caution as a form of what they call "self-stigma"—we know some people might reject us because of our diagnosis, and we therefore avoid reaching out. At age sixty-three, I'd frame that differently. I am often cautious in attempting new friendships because I am so experienced in relationship failure. Sometimes the failures have been clearly my fault. Bipolar disorder has a bad habit of taking a chainsaw to a person's relational bridges, then burning whatever's left of them. People with many kinds of mental health problems can behave erratically in ways that challenge friendships. We can drop out of sight for weeks, even months, at a time—sometimes because we're doing poorly, sometimes because we're well and focusing on work that we won't be able to do when we're more challenged. Friendships generally require consistency, among other kinds of nourishment, and we unintentionally undermine relationships by failing to feed them.

Many relationship failures are less clearly one-sided. It's part of our hardwired human nature to be skittish of people who make us feel uncomfortable. And people with mental health problems can make others uncomfortable. At one dinner party I hosted, a guest laughed so hard at her own potty humor that she fell from her chair onto the dining room floor. The other guests had their own idiosyncrasies, so no one was startled. At your dinner party, it might be a different story.

BELONGING IN CHRIST

Yet even as those with mental health challenges experience exclusion, we belong in Christ. In many ways, this is the most fundamental description of what it means to be a Christian.

Each Christian belongs to God. We belong to God's family. God chose us to belong, so we belong. And not only do we belong, but we cannot be made to un-belong. What the Father has given to Jesus cannot be taken from Jesus (John 10:29). We are so close to God it is as if each of us is engraved on the palms of God's hands (Isaiah 49:16).

Because we belong, God didn't just die for our sake; he carries us out of our darkness indelibly and forever engraved on his palms. God promises: "I will never leave you nor forsake you" (Joshua 1:5; see also Deuteronomy 31:6, 8; Hebrews 13:5). As we belong to God, so also are we members of God's household and family, a bond that cannot be broken. When we experience that secure place of belonging among God's people, we find a place that is "not just pleasant; it is life saving," Rosaria Butterfield writes. "Godly community is a sweet balm of safety. It gives us a place and a season where we are safe with ourselves and safe with others."[3]

FINDING BELONGING

Community can be hard to find. Belonging has been on the decline in the United States for decades. Robert Putnam's 2000 book *Bowling Alone* took the decline of league bowling as a central metaphor for the overall trend. This decline affects church membership, denominational affiliations, and membership in civic organizations like Rotary and in nonpartisan political groups such as the League of Women Voters. It even shows up, in Putnam's estimation, in how much less likely we are to share our evening meal with family (down by a third over two decades) or play cards with friends (down nearly two-thirds).[4]

It may not be coincidental that in the same period, there has been a remarkable rise in diagnoses related to social difficulties: from social anxiety disorder to autism spectrum disorder. Social anxiety disorder is what happens when what we might think of as "shyness" has escalated to a life-impeding fear of social settings. People with social anxiety may experience a racing heart, shaking, blushing, breathlessness, and the overwhelming certainty that others will judge or publicly humiliate them.[5] Today, more than 7 percent of the US population experiences social anxiety in a year, and more than 12 percent are projected to experience it over their lifetime.[6]

Autism spectrum disorder describes a range of conditions. Various difficulties in social settings are typical, along with unusually high focus on topics of interest; extreme sensitivity to light, sound, and touch; and repetitive behaviors that may extend from self-comforting to self-harming. Since 2004, the rate of autism spectrum diagnoses in the United States has more than tripled to one child in fifty-four in 2020, according to the Centers for Disease Control and Prevention.[7] This, along with the growth in social anxiety, suggests that a growing portion of those who could become part of congregations will have difficulty making the attachments to other people that are core to our sense of belonging in the body.

Church isn't always an easy place to experience belonging. I found a clear sense of belonging for the first time after more than three decades attending church as an adult, and it wasn't at church. It was in my Rotary club.

Rotary is a civic organization with a hundred-year-old meeting ritual and a commitment to engage every member in "service above self." Rotary gave me a place to go, tasks to do, and a predictable structure. Those things made it easier for me to feel like I belonged. Once I'd experienced belonging at Rotary, it was easier to identify a church that felt the same. I chose a congregation with liturgical worship, a choir that functioned as what some newer churches call a life group, validation of my volunteer work as a chaplain, and lots of optional scheduled activities.

While my church belonging has characteristics similar to my civic engagement, belonging to a church is categorically different from belonging to a civic organization. It's different theologically: in the church, I am organically joined to a body, of which I am an essential member. I may be as invisible and as rarely considered as a bile duct, but I'm no less essential to the body's effective functioning.

Research, too, hints that church belonging affects us differently than other kinds of belonging. A multinational European study published in 2015 is tantalizing. The researchers assessed how well different vehicles for community engagement helped older adults in ten countries elude depression over seven years. People joined all kinds of community organizations to find connections: sports clubs, political associations, hobbyist groups. The researchers found the most effective depression preventive was engagement in communities of faith.[8] In fact, Mauricio Avendano, a research epidemiologist who coauthored the study, said that the mental health benefits of belonging to political and community organizations were only short term.[9]

What makes belonging to communities of faith different? Could it be that faith communities provide not just a place to belong, but an enduring identity and a purpose in belonging? Sports clubs and political organizations may face disappointing reverses, but in the words of the familiar hymn, "God's

truth abideth still." God is "a mighty fortress" in whose presence we find a place of hope and belonging that cannot be
destroyed.[10]

The enduring purpose that our community of God provides
resonates with the kind of people who find belonging when
there's something for them to do. Some of the simplest, old-
line congregational management tools allow members and
attenders to experience this kind of purpose:

- *Call trees* give a large portion of the congregation
  responsibility for sharing information and an opportunity to experience belonging as they connect to pass
  along messages.
- *Meal sharing* among members of the congregation—
  even ordinary Sunday or weeknight dinners—allows the
  isolated to experience belonging with others.
- *Visiting shut-ins* provides a reminder that they still
  belong, and gives those who visit the chance to belong
  together with them.

Those who are isolated are often shut out of belonging with
the unhelpful mental health myth "You can't give what you
don't have." In practice this means that people who are lonely
are excluded from companioning ministries on the ground
that they'd be serving from their lack, not their abundance.
To which I say: Those without companions absolutely need
to give companionship. And those who enter ministry aware
of their own lack can be all the more ready to let God fill the
empty places.

We know who we are when we belong. The idea that we
should each, as individuals, establish our own identity separate from established community relationships is new and

remains unusual. Scottish theologian John Swinton writes, "In a very real sense we are persons-in-relation. . . . I am only a father because of my children, a husband because of my wife, a lecturer because of my occupation."[11] That is to say, each of us finds our identity in the places and relationships where we allow ourselves to belong. I am a Christian, a Rotarian, a Mainer, part of the Hill family, a fundraiser, a gardener, and a writer. These identities depend on my association with and acceptance by the various communities of my belonging.

I cannot know I belong to God unless I belong among God's people. Jesus prayed that we would be one with him and the Father, as he and the Father were one, so that the world would know that he was the beloved Son of the Father (John 17:21). Our ability to live together as those who belong to God and to one another is a primary test of our faith in God. Do we believe that God could have chosen an individual who doesn't readily fit in? Do we trust that God can keep us safe from a person whose differences cause us fear? Do we believe that God can work through a person whose eccentricities cause us discomfort?

To accomplish the things God has charged us to do requires us to live in unity, as God has called us to live. To do that demands that we break down a wide range of human-created barriers to connection and belonging. When we talk about barriers that separate us from those with mental health problems, the phrase we often use to describe these barriers is the "stigma associated with mental illnesses."

WHAT IS STIGMA, AND WHY IS IT SO HARD TO OVERCOME?

In his 1963 book *Stigma: Notes on the Management of Spoiled Identity*, Erving Goffman describes *stigma* as a social function that defines some individuals or groups as unacceptable to the community. Stigma, he says, is assigned on the basis of character (he includes unemployment and mental illness in this classification), physical deformities, or membership in a suspect group (such as those related to race, ethnicity, or religion). It's a powerful tool that defines who can be in and who must be out. It exists because it is useful in establishing a community's boundaries. Stigma sets outside the community those whose differences would endanger the community, thereby protecting the community's core identity. But stigma can also set outside the community those whose differences are only believed to be dangerous: immigrants, people of color, people of a different religious heritage, people with mental health problems.

The nature of stigma helps explain how a quarter century of campaigns to "break the stigma of mental illness" exist alongside continuing increases in stigma against people with mental illnesses.[12] The campaigns have tried to break stigma by presenting biological explanations of mental health problems. They urge us to understand that these behaviors and difficult emotional states are the result of an individual's fixed and unchanging biology. They are not the person's fault!

But when an intrinsic, unchanging, and unchangeable condition is the basis for differentiating among people, the difference easily becomes stigmatized. In *The Stigma Effect*, psychologist Patrick Corrigan summarizes several decades of research into stigma and stigma-busting campaigns.[13] He analyzes three models of anti-stigma campaign that have been popular over the last thirty years and says the evidence shows that the most popular strategies simply don't work:

- Educational campaigns raise even higher the existing barriers between the stigmatized group and the public. These campaigns provide information that reminds people of all the ways the stigmatized group is, in fact, different. Mental health educational campaigns typically assert that those with mental health problems are fundamentally different in their DNA and basic biology. Identifying a group as fundamentally different creates stigma instead of alleviating it.

- Advocacy campaigns are generally built by people who speak on behalf of those who are stigmatized. A celebrity advocates for her sister with mental health problems. A parent advocates for his child with mental health problems. A group of families advocate for better services for their loved ones. These campaigns tend to be run without the voices of people with mental health problems, continuing to leave us outside of the room. Advocacy tends to identify people with mental health problems as a social concern to be solved instead of valued members of our human community.

- Face-to-face encounters are, according to Corrigan, the way stigma disappears. In these direct encounters, it is possible for those with and without mental health problems to recognize each other's humanity and value.

Isn't that how we long to interact at church?

MAKING FRIENDS, BREAKING STIGMA

A 2018 study by Lifeway Research found that many people with mental health problems are longing for simple acceptance in their congregations. Among Protestants with a mental illness diagnosis, 70 percent wished others at church would get to know them as a friend. Those who attended church consistently were more likely to feel socially excluded: of these, 78 percent longed for church friends.[14]

Churches are inclined to admire, even idolize, people whose pain has been "endured with perfect grace, with perfect faith, and never succumbed to in weakness," comments memoirist Alia Joy.[15] People who can suffer silently and invisibly are welcome in any congregation, especially if they then lead ministries that care for other needy people. We're even more happy to honor pain once it has been healed.

Those of us whose long-lasting suffering limits our lives often have a different experience, in church as elsewhere. This is unfortunate, because when the body behaves as it is designed and called to function, our mental health problems can diminish to some degree. When people feel loved, cared for, and safe, our mental health symptoms may become less challenging. Sometimes the symptoms diminish. Sometimes they are just less overwhelming when we live in a warm community of people who care. Think again about how the COVID pandemic affected our national mental health. Depression and anxiety surged among folks who don't ordinarily experience them. The required social distancing isolated them from many ordinary sources of love and care, and they became emotionally unsettled. As we all figured out new ways to connect and care, we found better stability in the new normal.

There are understandable reasons why churches would set people with mental health problems at the margins. Some congregations fear being overwhelmed by our needs. Some are anxious about our potential to wield excessive and damaging influence. When churches organize outreach by a "like draws like" ministry model, they unintentionally select for those who have the most friends. That creates strong organizations, but not healthy congregations. God hasn't limited the body to those who match our current outgoing ideal of what's best.

Because God sees differently than we do, the body—as God intends it—looks different. And that different-looking body has an impact beyond what our wisdom imagines.

A friend who came to Christ as a college student in the conformist 1950s told me that part of what drew him to Jesus were the truly peculiar people he found mixed in among the mostly upper-crust members of the historic congregation he eventually joined. No merely social club would have ever allowed some of them to cross the threshold, much less participate, he said. That's what convinced him that something qualitatively different from social affinities drew people to this place. Eventually, he learned to recognize God as the drawing force.

When we allow our congregations to become segregated on the basis of differences, we also lose the blessings God intends to bestow through the people we shut out. When we select as "high potential" members only those who could help quickly multiply the congregation, we risk filling the community with what pediatric epidemiologist W. Thomas Boyce describes as "dandelions"—the kind of people who, like the bright summer flower, do all right under almost any conditions. But we're likely to miss what he calls "orchid" people—those whose lives are marked by extremely high potential for *both* outstanding contributions and catastrophic failure because of their extreme reactivity to their surroundings.

THE HEALING POWER OF FRIENDSHIP

Churches are called and gifted by God to be places of love, care, and belonging. When we live that out, we support all our congregation, including those who live with mental health challenges. We may even find ourselves—nonprofessionals that we are—uniquely capable of supporting those who struggle with mental health problems.

Medical school professor Peter Kramer points out that what makes any therapy successful is not the therapeutic model but the quality of the relationship between the patient and the counselor.[16] In other words, quality relationships help people achieve their best mental health. And the helper doesn't need to be current in the latest therapies. Helpers just need to stay committed to helping others grow into their own best success.

Churches are intended to be places where we live in relationship with God and one another. Those relationships are often difficult and demanding. The challenges our relationships pose help us grow in Christlikeness. In that sense, our Christian friendships can be described as moral enterprises. Pastoral theologian John Swinton describes friendship as a type of experiential theology that helps each of us grow in self-knowledge so we can continue to grow in virtue. Friendship, he says, "is a way of living that ensures that human beings can be enabled to live their lives humanly." These kinds of friendships can't be chosen "on the basis of likeness, utility or social exchange." Instead, they thrive in the world of "*solicitude*—the anxiety over the good of another [that is] fundamental to all moral behavior."[17]

Those caring friendships are transformative for people with mental health challenges. In an interview with the Shay Moral Injury Center, psychiatrist William Nash said that the people who are most likely to overcome mental health challenges are those who found relationships where "somebody listened to them, really listened . . . without becoming disgusted, without judging," and still loved them. For the sufferer to experience that love as genuine, Nash said, "it can't really be a helping professional like me who's paid to come in and give you 50 minutes of an hour."[18] The love that heals is not for sale.

WAYS TO BEFRIEND THOSE WITH MENTAL HEALTH PROBLEMS

A church that invites people with mental health challenges into the life of Christ is a church where everyone's in and everyone's essential. This comes relatively easy to a small congregation with limited resources, where to overlook anyone is to clearly leave something undone. It can be more difficult in a large, pastor-centered church where interchangeable volunteers simply fulfill tasks on the leadership's checklist. In a welcoming congregation, each person is noticed, and everyone knows they matter. Everyone's invited. No one is left to navigate their own way to activities and relationships. Personal invitations are generous, and public information is easily available via bulletin boards, websites, and other forums. If you want to attend a Bible study, you know when it happens and who to call, text, or email. If you want to support the local teen center, you can easily locate the list of needed items and where to leave them.

A welcoming congregation provides places for ministry. It can be hard to recognize that people on the margins have divine callings with the potential to bless a congregation and the world at large. Because of my work, I've known many people with intellectual disabilities whose congregations have welcomed them in service. One was an usher; two drummed and danced on their Sunday worship team. One writes poems of spiritual encouragement for new believers. Another is training to share retreat leadership with her mother, and still another bakes the best coffee hour cookies I have ever eaten.

The late John Cacioppo and his research team at the University of Chicago did some fascinating work about ways to battle the loneliness that threatens to overwhelm our culture. One finding: lonely individuals should be given opportunities to engage in acts of kindness and generosity because through the "social norm of reciprocity," these acts are likely to generate "gratitude, mutual respect, cooperation, trust, and stronger bonds."[19] The gifts economy framework offers another useful explanation (see chapter 6). When we allow others to give from their giftedness, we become relationally bound to each other in the gifts-based economy of grace. And those bound in relationship experience belonging and find hope.

This means that to wrap a congregation together in the fruitful relationship of giving and receiving requires welcoming gifts from all. Pastors who are inclined to push aside congregants whose mental health problems make them more difficult, hear this. To tell us that "you can't give what you don't have" and set us on the sideline until we meet your standard for godliness (or pleasantness) makes our condition worse, not better. The person who is alone or left out can't get companionship without trying to give it. As our grandmothers might have told us, the way to have a friend is to be one.

In the secular disability services agency where I work now, our first teacher looked at each new student with a simple affirmation and question: "God, you sent this person to us. What do we do with this person?"[20] Not "What do we do *for* this person?" or "How do we *fix* this person?" but "What do we do [together] *with* this person?" The very phrasing describes a commitment to be together and serve together, in a way that describes the authentic togetherness we are to have in the body of Christ.

Although mental health problems can be as limiting as more obvious disabilities, they don't eliminate the God-built drive to serve. Because of the associated stigma, we sometimes may not know about the mental illness of people who are serving in our congregations. I think of one Sunday school director who kept her diagnosis under wraps for years out of concern that anyone who knew she had a mental illness would not trust her with their children.

A welcoming congregation also provides support for needs. We know that God urges us to "strengthen the feeble hands, steady the knees that give way; say to those with fearful hearts, 'Be strong, do not fear'" (Isaiah 35:3-4). When we invite those on the margins into our congregations, we need to listen well enough to understand and serve their specific needs. How do we do that?

Most often, we help in the same ways we help anyone.

- *Isolated people need companionship*—not just at church events, but throughout the week. A ministry of visitation or a team of visiting deacons will support their need to be part of the community, whether they're isolated because of temporary illness, permanent disability, extreme shyness, or a diagnosed mental health problem. Believe it or not, simply touching base regularly is an evidence-based strategy for preventing suicide.[21] Your congregation's ordinary habit of regularly calling, visiting, and sending notes to those who are housebound is an evidence-based mental health practice robust enough to help prevent suicides, the worst of all mental illness outcomes.

- *Caregivers need respite*—and this includes not just married parents who enjoy a church-supported "date night" or stay-at-home moms who attend a weekday Bible study. The congregant who provides full-time care to an adult child who is disabled or a mentally ill spouse needs a break. The single working parent needs a break. The "sandwich generation" individuals caring for both their own kids and their aging parent need a break. Sometimes these can be organized as group activities. Often, care-givers' demanding schedules require one-on-one respite in their own home by someone who has learned their needs by being attentive to them.

- *Those without transportation need rides*—to church events, medical appointments, and more. Does the church organize rides? Do people commonly offer? Because of relatively low incomes, people with serious mental health problems are among those less likely to have ready transportation access. On my second visit to a small church in Maine, I was asked if I could provide a ride to a member of the church who lived nearer to me than to any member. In this one request, it offered belonging both for the member who had trouble getting to Sunday services and for the newcomer who needed a way to connect.

- *Those with limiting conditions need accommodations to make church activities accessible*—perhaps desirable space in the sanctuary for wheelchairs and walkers. Maybe hearing assistance for those with impairments or a quieter place for those who can't bear the roar of a contemporary worship band. Shy or socially anxious people might need routes into service projects or small groups that don't require making a face-to-face request to join.[22]

Sometimes the best supports happen quietly and privately. That's how I was supported more than a decade ago after a new medication sparked a terrifying delusion in me. I suddenly became convinced that God was evil and the Bible a pack of lies. I'm grateful that I retained enough sense not to blurt this out in my women's Bible study or small group. But when my long-standing prayer partner Cecelia and I met, I dared to tell her. She thought a moment, then said, "You haven't always believed this. I'm quite sure you won't always believe it. But while you do believe it, you don't need to pray. I'll pray on your behalf." She ensured that I maintained a sense of belonging among God's people even when I wasn't able to participate in the most basic of its rituals, speaking with our God.

In the same way that Cecelia could see me, not just my symptoms, welcoming congregations see people. As noted earlier, professor Patrick Corrigan's research on mental health stigma found that the most effective antidote is face-to-face relationships between members of the stigmatized group and others. That is to say: the fellowship many of us intend to offer in our churches is an evidence-based practice for breaking mental health stigma. In the words of the song many of us learned in children's church or around campfires, "they will know we are Christians by our love" for all those among us.

In practical terms, what might this look like?

- *See humanity first, differences second.* Framing conversations around common experiences helps welcome other people whose lives differ in some specifics. Not everyone has children, but almost everyone has cared about some people in a place where they have lived. Most people do something during their waking hours, although not everyone goes to work or school. Ask "How do you spend your days?" rather than "What do you do for work?"
- *Create a church that functions as a family,* not as a cluster of marketing target groups. As church communities develop mental health ministries, it can be easy to shunt people with mental health problems aside into special

rooms with special workbooks and special recovery liturgies, limiting us to only each other's companionship. Being welcomed as a new marketing target isn't always the same as being invited to full membership in the family of God.

- *Live with differences.* Most congregations already welcome some differences of opinion and lifestyle. We include people who never fail to attend and soccer families who disappear on Sundays during the season. We welcome families and individuals on both sides of the political aisle. Can we manage to include people for whom even an ordinary conversation might be challenging? I remember an ice-breaker question about favorite movie actors. It was so far from my world that I was speechless. Could you graciously give a pass without later avoiding the awkward attender?

- *Be ready to receive the gift the guest brings,* however small or flawed. One reason local people in need value the monthly brunch at my church is that they can participate as equals. At our brunch, everyone who has something to bring, does. Some of us bake a specialty; some bring something from the supermarket. Those with limited means bring a dozen hard-boiled eggs or a small box of cold cereal. They share as everyone shares, except at greater personal cost. The small, and sometimes erratic, contributions to community life from those with mental health problems are likewise given from their limited resources and deserve the same welcome as larger gifts.

SMALL BEGINNINGS: INTENTIONALLY END ISOLATION

People left alone are vulnerable to every kind of difficulty: not just loneliness and anxiety, but material challenges, mental health problems, and many kinds of sin. Congregations can create opportunities for people to be in the company of others: group activities, small group activities, one-on-one prayer partnerships. Various systems for touching base ensure members of the congregation don't feel alone: phone trees, prayer chains, letter and card writing, email greetings. During the coronavirus pandemic, congregations became very creative in providing options, including daily prayer via FaceTime and coffee hour on Zoom. Offer opportunities for fun, for meal sharing, for spiritual uplift and understanding.

People are often left out accidentally because we're in the habit of doing things in the ways most comfortable for ourselves. Some people, including those with long- or short-term mental health problems, may not have ordinary social skills. It helps to structure the church environment to afford us a welcome anyway. As one example: many contemporary congregations are structured around "relational ministry"—the idea that people find their connections and opportunities through the casual interactions of coffee hour and Bible group "fellowship" time. This approach excludes those who find group activity difficult. Similarly, if people are expected to call the church office to sign up for activities, the congregation is unlikely to offer belonging to those of God's people who experience social anxiety. Simply posting opportunities and sign-up sheets in a public place—whether a bulletin board or a website—is far more likely to afford a sense of welcome to those less socially adept.[23]

Likewise, congregations where small groups typically reorganize every few months can still include long-term activities that function as small groups for those who don't handle relationship transitions readily. The choir is that group in my current congregation; I know another church where Celebrate Recovery serves that purpose.

Helping people belong can require rethinking our own social habits as well. Who is invited to Sunday dinner after church? One family, new to town, determined that they would always invite to Sunday lunch whoever was sitting nearest them in church. Their first guest gasped in gratitude: "I've been attending here for three years and no one has ever asked me to lunch," the woman said. Another family committed to inviting guests three Sundays a month. After two years and just a handful of reciprocal invitations, they gave up. No one seemed to understand that belonging together takes effort from everyone involved.

THE CHALLENGE

The biggest challenge is to find the sweet spot between welcoming people with mental health challenges as we are and still encouraging us to become the best we can be. This is similar to the challenge we all live as we seek to grow in Christlikeness. Churches are designed to be communities that develop the character of Christ in people. We aren't designed to modify people's biological weaknesses.

But the more we focus on diagnoses, the more difficult this can become. Diagnoses, especially amateur diagnoses, easily become tools for dismissing others. I've become particularly concerned with how readily we label others as "toxic" or "narcissists" and erect self-protective boundaries instead of discipling. Back in the day, we'd have labeled the so-called narcissist a "self-centered so-and-so," and presumed there was both room for and reasonable expectation of the kinds of growth that churches nurture.[24] When we let ourselves define others by their difficulties, as if these are immutable, we excise God and ourselves from the transforming work God empowers people to do.

For those of us struggling with mental health problems, the belief that mental health challenges are intractable, lifelong conditions can make it feel like a battle just to maintain a sense of dignity, let alone achieve ordinary life goals: an income, a family, a home, a circle of friends, a church home. It can also make it difficult for others to welcome the sufferer whose challenges may never cease to challenge.

THE GOOD NEWS

The good news is that belonging, in itself, is remarkably restorative to mental health, and belonging is something the church is uniquely called, equipped, and even commanded to nurture. A meta-analysis of sixty-four studies from 1996 to 2015 found that social support alone "makes a measurable improvement in the lives of people with mental illness."[25] The isolation that people with mental health problems experience both results from and adds to our difficulties. People avoid us because we're different, and we become more different because we're often excluded from the mediating benefits of living as members of the human community.

Living in the community of God's people establishes that my life has meaning not just to an abstract and intangible God but to the very body of Christ to which God has called me. It offers the experience of purposeful living as I meet my obligations to my congregation and as my congregation helps me understand how to live all the other hours of my week. Within the body I may find a place where I am allowed to belong, however limited my experience of belonging elsewhere. I may also find that my own inclination to difficult behaviors is moderated by the experience of attuning to the larger group's ordinariness. As US surgeon general Vivek Murthy explains, drawing on the work of neuroscientist Matthew Lieberman, "our identities absorb the influences of others like social sponges."[26] Surrounded by people in relatively better mental health, I am not just encouraged by their example to live in healthier ways; I am far less likely to make unhealthy choices.

The good news is that belonging stabilizes mental health. And while stigma can impede belonging, belonging is, in itself, the best way to remove stigma. As professor Patrick Corrigan points out, education and advocacy are far less effective in overcoming people's fear about mental health problems than are face-to-face relationships with those with mental health diagnoses. And this is what your congregation's strategy of welcome can provide: both the belonging that stabilizes mental health and the relationships that make mental health challenges less fearful.

6

Finding Value in Challenged Lives

Worth . . . is given to each person by the way that others, including—and ultimately—God, regard him or her.

—**DAVID PAILIN**, *A Gentle Touch—From a Theology of Handicap to a Theology of Human Being*

What is a human life worth? What makes my own life worthwhile? Is my time valuable only when my efforts add up to some measurable achievement I can document on my résumé or in my exercise log or my family's "brag book"? And if that's the case, what value is there to a less productive life? To the less productive moments in any life?

Answering those questions forces us to examine our deepest values and commitments. For those who grew up in the Christians faith, we learned from our earliest days in children's church that God sees every life as priceless. God urges us to see one another as irreplaceable members of God's body. We are not free to disregard anyone, because all are essential to the whole. We must all rely on each other, and all of us together rely on God. God created us; God's Spirit is the wind carrying us forward, and God's Son empowers forgiveness of our failings, which are many.

Still, we are often prone to value our productivity—what we can create—over our identity as God's creations, even when we're trying to create work for God in this world. To maximize our measurable contributions, we often overlook contributions and contributors that don't fit our preconceived plans for success. We also can find it hard to obey God's command to rest. God directly commands us to reserve one day in seven to rest, and we are humbled to live in bodies that God created to require many hours of rest daily. Some of us, including many of us with mental health problems, are further humbled to live in bodies that must rest far more than others.

When we acknowledge that God has given value to each of God's people, we are better able to recognize that God values even the sometimes less productive lives of those with mental health problems. And when we acknowledge that God has given value to rest, it becomes easier to allow ourselves and others the rest we need, instead of rushing from task to task in our own attempts to create value in God's valuable created world.

HOW DO WE VALUE A HUMAN LIFE?

Market economies like ours assign their own value to almost everything. That's the nature of a market economy. It establishes value in measurable exchange equivalents according to whatever currency that market uses. Cowries or coins, it doesn't matter. The values can fluctuate over time and circumstance, but there will be values set.

Dominant market economies are relatively new on the world scene. For most of history, people have lived in complex webs of relationship and obligation that anthropologists describe as gift economies. In a gift economy, each shares from their own abundance and becomes relationally connected by the responsibility to make a later return gift. The value of the reciprocal gift may not be equivalent. It may demonstrate by its limits or lavishness the disparity in social status between parties. The establishment of relative social status is, in itself, part of the relational nature of the gift economy.[1]

We see this gift economy enacted in the biblical accounts of the temple feasts, where people bring their gifts to the temple to honor God, and the king and Levites, as representatives of God, reciprocate with gifts of festive foods to all those gathered. The gifts vary by individual ability to contribute; the return varies by household size. The value of the giving is to bind all together in a community of honor and thanks.[2]

A gift economy is more profoundly demonstrated in the relationship with God we gain through our relationship with Jesus. Jesus makes the gift of his life to us. We return whatever relatively small and insignificant gifts of gratitude we are able to provide. God the Father gives the gift of forgiveness. We return our entirely inadequate thanks and our inconsistent willingness to share that forgiveness with others who have offended us. God the Spirit gives the manifold gifts that empower our lives and service. We return our thanks by using those gifts to benefit all the people of God. In all these gifts and return giving, God and people bind the community of faith together in honor, thanks, and service.

In a gift economy, the value of a life is measured by its generosity to others. The Queen of Sheba shows honor to King Solomon with generous gifts of gold, precious stones, and such spices as "there had never been." Solomon responds by giving the queen "more than she had brought to him" (2 Chronicles 9:9, 12), affirming her generosity in praise of his rule by demonstrating even greater generosity to her. In a converse example, the wealthy herdsman Nabal loses social place (and nearly loses his life) by failing to demonstrate generosity toward David and his men after they have protected Nabal's flocks. Nabal is described as "wicked" and a "fool" for his failure to respond generously to their generous gift of service (1 Samuel 25).

Generosity is not a measure our US market economy, government, or legal systems use when trying to decide how much a life is worth. They ask different questions. Is a child's life (with its many years of unknown potential) worth more or less than the remaining life of a retired adult? Is the life of a working man worth more than that of a working woman? A stay-at-home mom? An unemployed man? An adult whose disability prevents them from working? Is the life of a White person worth more than a Black person? Is a life worth more if it's given in service by soldiers or first responders? These questions play out in how we assign cash value to lives for medical insurance, life and disability insurance, wrongful death and injury lawsuits, survivors' compensation, and risk-benefit assessments for safety regulations.

When we thus measure lives in dollars, we make people objects in trade, not persons in relationship. We are treating them, in the language of Austrian Jewish theologian Martin Buber, as "it" and not "thou." We remove their God-assigned inherent value from the equation and replace it with our human assignment of market value, ceasing to celebrate God's gracious gifts through them to all of us.

FINDING GOD'S VALUE IN ALL LIVES

Theology and philosophy distinguish between relationships that are *transactional* and those rooted in *love*. Transactional relationships are like those of the market economies, defined by the metered back-and-forth flow of equivalent benefits between the two parties. A love-based relationship can be two-way, but the nature of compassion means that its benefits accrue unequally to the parties from time to time. The relationship between a family and their paid childcare worker is transactional. The family's children are looked after; the worker gets compensated for his time. The relationship between a sleep-deprived mother and her nursing infant is different. The infant gets nourishment without which it would not survive. Mom sometimes wonders if she'll survive another early morning feeding. Here, the relationship depends on love.[3]

God's relationship with us is the ultimate in non-transactional relationships. God expects no equivalent return from relationship with me, yet God, out of love, makes me not just a member of the household but a friend. Pastoral theologian John Swinton suggests that God also calls us to similarly non-transactional friendships within our congregations and beyond, in imitation of God's friendship with us. For those in Christ, our relationships are not supposed to depend on how appealing or useful we find each other. Our relationships in Christ are intended to reflect "passion, commitment, solidarity, the desire to be *with* and *for* the other," and to demonstrate the character of God's relationship with us, where servants have become friends.[4]

Friendship expert Shasta Nelson says it's important to recognize that relationships that challenge us are both more essential to forming the communities we desire and more tolerable than we sometimes think. Not every irritating behavior is toxic. It's irritating to be the one who most often initiates contact, but if the friend demonstrates in other ways that she values the relationship, that doesn't need to be a deal-breaker. It's wearing to be the equanimous Christopher Robin to another's Eeyore. But if you value the other person, this doesn't have to mean it's time to break bonds.[5] It's valid to set differences aside and simply connect to the human value God has placed in those God places around us. Even those whose mental health problems confuse, irritate, or upset us. Again, in Swinton's words: "The priority of friends is the personhood of the other, not the illness."[6]

To value the personhood of an individual with mental health challenges requires paying more attention to God's creative work in the person than to the ways that creation has been marred. And there are definitely times when that can be hard to do. It's easy to see God in the person with a serious mental health diagnosis when he's praying daily with his pastor for their church plant. More difficult are the times when that person becomes lost in delusion and self-endangerment. It's relatively easy to see God in the voice that breaks out in original worship song during the Sunday service. It's more difficult when the music is banged on an out-of-tune guitar sometime after midnight on the other side of a too-thin apartment wall.

To value others for their personhood also requires believing that God so loved the person you see now—just as she is—that God was willing to sacrifice his Son on that person's behalf, just as he did for us. And that God may have sent the Spirit already to indwell the person, despite the obvious imperfections, just as the Spirit indwells us despite our imperfections.

When we understand the value God sees in ourselves and others, we can rest. We don't need to try to be something different or to make others be different, because we know that we and they are already enough.

WE ALL NEED REST

Hard work and achievement are part of our American cultural DNA. But over time, that drive has metastasized into something less laudable and more life-threatening. In the last hundred years, we've trimmed more than a quarter of our average nightly sleep hours in the United States—from 9 hours in 1910 to 6.8 in 2013.[7] We're trying to live as if our bodies were not created with built-in limits, and it's endangering us.

The correlations between short sleep and bad health are overwhelming. Science tells us that those who sleep less than seven hours a night are 30–50 percent more likely to suffer a stroke, chronic kidney disease, heart attack or coronary heart disease, arthritis, or asthma.[8] But even knowing that sleep is essential to our health, we're inclined to balance the risks against the rewards (sleep more/work less? sleep less/scroll more?) and to choose against sleep.

Most of us know that we get cranky when we don't have enough sleep. We aren't able to perform our best at work or at home. Medical research tells us that sleep is foundational to good health. We also may recognize that our spiritual life suffers when we don't rest adequately. Steve Macchia, who teaches spiritual formation for church leaders, reminds us that when we fail to get enough rest, our souls become unhealthy and spiritually vulnerable, just as lack of rest creates easily recognized vulnerabilities in our health, performance, and emotions.[9]

Many kinds of mental health problems are exacerbated by sleeplessness. For those who aren't inclined to mental health problems, snappishness or lack of focus might be a signal that more downtime is needed. For those with mental illness diagnoses, sleeplessness can be a symptom of or precursor to difficult times. Extended periods of sleeplessness can be a symptom of depression. One friend with schizophrenia is likely to fall into paranoid delusions after a few anxious nights awake. For those like me with bipolar diagnoses, a period of creative enthusiasm can launch into a multiday binge of activity that literally never stops until the body either crashes or swings dangerously high.

God designed our bodies to require rest, and rest is remedy and restoration for every human body. Writer and pastor Joyce Hollyday was surprised to discover among the impoverished residents of Latin American refugee camps "committees of joy" that reprimanded missionaries for their endless hours of work. Working nonstop was a sure sign the missionaries were short-timers, the committees said. Without play and celebration, they would never sustain important work over the long haul.[10]

Restorative rest can come even in the brief break of a meal taken away from work and among friends. Dietrich Bonhoeffer describes these breaks as reminders of God's own Sabbath rest: "Our life is not only travail and labor; it is also refreshment and joy in the goodness of God. . . . Through our daily meals He is calling us to rejoice, to keep holiday in the midst of our working day."[11]

Rest is one of the ways by which we are re-created. It is also a way in which we acknowledge and value our own true and finite selves. Resting is one of the ways we demonstrate daily that we know our accomplishments are not fully our own. God works in and through us to accomplish God's own purposes. And God is able to accomplish those goals with or without our 24/7 involvement. God can do this even in the face of our human limitations, which have not escaped the attention of the All-Seeing One.

A tenth-century Roman Catholic pope expressed this humble trust in his bedtime prayer: "I've done the best I could in your service this day. Oh Lord, I'm going to bed. It's your church. Take care of it!"[12]

How often do we need to remind ourselves: This is God's world. We live here by God's gracious gift. Because none of us is God, we don't have God's responsibility. We're responsible for only as much as God has assigned each of us. And God can certainly manage during our times of rest.

The particular mental health problems I have require me to rest more than many people do. My need for rest gives me something in common with friends who live with physical disabilities. They, too, often need to choose between what they want to do and what their bodily limits allow. They, too, sometimes find that their challenges place boundaries around their ambitions and dreams.

It's important for all of us to acknowledge the limits we experience in this world. All of us—those with more challenges and those with fewer challenges—make our offerings from within our own specific limits. And we all are to be grateful together for what God has made us, individually and together.

The rest that restores any one of us relates to the unique design God has created in us. Introverts are, of course, restored by time away from people; extroverts by gatherings with people. People who love to do things may find that they rest best by doing something different from their everyday activities. Volunteer work as a health center chaplain refreshes me from my weekday job as a fundraiser. For a professional chaplain, refreshment is likely to take quite different forms.

People who live with mental health problems face some distinct challenges in finding quality rest. First is the difficulty some experience in resting at all. Sleep is a challenge from time to time across a wide range of mental health problems—anxiety, depression, manias, and even psychotic disorders.

Choosing refreshing activities is also challenging for some, especially people who are in a depression. I remember one outing to a lush and lovely city park with a friend who was struggling. My friend grumbled through the entire day of picnicking, riding the carousel, feeding the ducks, and pedaling the paddleboats. A few hours after we dropped him off at his home, he called. "Hey, that was kinda fun," he said. It had taken not just the full day but several additional hours for his heart to register that he'd had a good time.

When we're in the throes of a mental health problem, we have to choose to do things that we enjoy when we're in other states of mind, because in those moments nothing will appeal. For me, the best choices often are those that carry intrinsic rewards. Cooking a favorite recipe or baking something to share are favorite activities and also help build relationships. A long drive to a lake where I can rent a kayak or to a forest where trails will lead to a waterfall are other activities I choose to do when I'm trying to pull myself out of the depths.

As a person with a bipolar rushing brain, I also find that for me the best kinds of rest involve the opportunity to refocus. Physical activities like dance aerobics, gardening, practicing piano scales, kayaking, and nature photography engage multiple senses in a specific moment and help replace internal chaos with external order. Those are some specific ways God helps me find rest.

Churches can find it hard to encourage rest. Even our congregational attempts at recreation easily become large events to organize. Just thinking about them makes us tired. And still we understand that people who live in ways that exhaust them will not share God's good and abundant life with others. Instead, they'll feel drained of any abundant life they might have shared.

For congregations to encourage rest and refreshment often means to encourage all to do whatever is restful and refreshing to them, whenever they need it. When we are tempted to ask for yet more service from ones who today seem hesitant, we can release them in the knowledge there will be other chances for them to serve. And perhaps to tell them so directly: "There will be another chance. We'll miss you, but if this isn't a great time for you, do what you need to do. You know best." In God's grace, the person who accepts God's generous gift of rest is refreshed to later give generously to others.

SMALL BEGINNINGS: LOOK FOR WHAT GOD SEES

Being captivated by visible strengths—especially the ones associated with professional and ministry success—is one of the ways that congregations are lured away from welcoming those whose value is less obvious. People with wealth, worldly power, and the skills to back them up can get things done in the congregation, as in the world, and it's easy to value their gifts. Nonetheless, God has placed gifts in even the most challenged members of the flock, and they are there for the benefit of God's people. "God has put the body together, giving greater honor to the parts that lacked it, so that there should be no division in the body, but that its parts should have equal concern for each other" (1 Corinthians 12:24-25). In other words, God gives the greatest gifts to those who would otherwise be most likely to be overlooked. The people our culture writes off for their lack of achievements are likely to be those in whom God has planted the greatest value. Ask yourself, *What is God seeing that I'm not?* And when God answers, find a way to honor the message. A note of gratitude for what you see could be a start. An opportunity for them to share that gift could come next.

THE CHALLENGE

A person who lives with mental health challenges is always tempted to strive longer and harder in the hope of accomplishing more nearly what others do. In an online and globalized community, our lives easily become 24/7/365, and even our churches can become part of that activity treadmill. It's awfully easy to turn our worship into work. We test our sermon by its audience metrics and measure the gathering by its attendance count or—in an old-line congregation—by the number of Bibles in the room. We arrive early to set up, stay through a service, a class, and a fellowship hour, count the offering, clean up the coffee table, and collect visitor response cards for follow up. Our day of rest can look anything but restful.

Contentment isn't easily accepted in our striving culture. Ethicist Christine Pohl notes, "Our cultural emphases on growth and success tend to undermine gratitude and to interpret contentment as an absence of drive or vision."[13] Those of us with mental health challenges need to live in gratitude and contentment, valuing the lives we experience in our communities of faith. Those without mental health challenges also need to live in gratitude and contentment, valuing the lives they experience as well as the lives they share with others. Those of us with mental health problems need to agree with God about our own need for rest. Those without mental health problems might learn from observing us that they, too, have their own need for rest, and that rest is a way to protect—not waste—the value God places in us.

THE GOOD NEWS

The quietness and rest that people with mental health problems need is also something we all need. In this regard, people with mental health problems—as well as those living with other challenging conditions—could be seen as reminders, or even sometimes as red warning lights, to Christians in the twenty-first-century West. Most of us require more stillness than our cultures are generally willing to give. For us to live according to the pace and drive of contemporary Western culture is for us to burn through our neural circuitry in ways that lead to disruptive and disorderly crises. For us to honor God with our lives, we need to live in ways that may seem out of step with many around us. Our most God-honoring ways of life may seem to gum up the rapidly moving machinery of busy churches. Still, God says every one of us has value. The person who must often rest is of value. So is the person who lives endlessly in rapid motion. In fact, that very active person's energy can help move burdens that are bringing others to a dead stop. It's countercultural to bear one another's burdens. It means one person's progress may be slowed to another person's pace so we all may finish together well. But this is the kind of life against culture that Christians have been called to from the beginning. As Paul urged the early church at Rome: "We who are strong ought to bear with the failings of the weak and not to please ourselves" (Romans 15:1).

Christians are called to nurture value in those the culture won't value—people with disabilities, children not yet born, people who learn slowly, people whose excess energy can be disruptive, those who live in poverty, those who find themselves imprisoned, those stunned by grief. To God, a person's value is in their personhood, not their productivity. God looks at the person less able to produce on their own and sees in that individual both a beloved part of God's very inheritance and an opportunity for service by others using the gifts and talents God has lovingly placed in that person.

The good news is this: people with mental health problems are a sign that God values all that God has created, even those parts of creation that carry signs of the fall. We are a sign that God has work still to be done in this world. And those of us with mental health problems, as well as those who live with other limits and challenges, are a sign that God calls not just us, but all of us, to rest.

7

Finding Feelings, Finding Hope

Where there are friends there is hope.

—**JOHN SWINTON,** *Resurrecting the Person*

I began writing this chapter from my home office during the coronavirus shutdown. We started relearning lots of things in this crisis: how to help each other, how to stay out of each other's way, how to make time for each other, how to entertain ourselves. I began sewing a few protective masks, in the process rediscovering my limited competence at the sewing machine. I was taught to "measure twice, cut once." Having measured twice, I still ended up with elastic that's too long as often as not.

Another thing many of us learned and continue to learn is that under unusual and threatening circumstances, we come under threat from uncomfortable feelings. In the first weeks of self-isolation, mental health experts alerted us to what they described as a rising tide of anxiety and depression. Less than a month into lockdown, the *Journal of the American Medical Association Internal Medicine* warned that disasters like the COVID-19 pandemic typically lead to various mental health consequences, including PTSD, depression, substance abuse, anxiety, and stress.[1]

The idea that emotions run high and dark in a crisis seems reasonable. It would be peculiar not to be stressed in an environment that is potentially hazardous to the survival of your loved ones. It would be inhuman not to feel distressed when forbidden to visit a dying parent in the nursing home. It would be abnormal not to be anxious about whether it's really possible to do a full-time job from a cramped apartment where your spouse is also trying to do a full-time job and one child is attempting to do full-time, online education while the preschooler keeps bursting into your Zoom room.

In other words, the huge and difficult feelings we experienced during and after COVID could be, for the most part, reasonable responses to the huge and difficult circumstances we shared.

SO MANY FEELINGS! SO LITTLE HOPE!

People raced through an entire encyclopedia of emotions in the first months of the coronavirus pandemic. Enthusiasm for long overlooked home improvement projects was quickly supplanted by a sense of frustration and tension as the number of new demands rose—demands for which we were mostly unprepared.

Still, it all seemed possible for the first month or two. Then two months became four, and then eight. Some people accustomed to meeting their own needs met hunger for the first time. Long-standing habits of hard work failed to serve, surfacing helplessness and hopelessness unfamiliar to many in the United States. And with the nature of the pandemic, even those with the healthiest lifestyles could no longer be confident in their futures. The only person at my workplace to become infected in the first six months was a classic fitness fanatic. If we could not be sure of life itself, then liberty and the pursuit of happiness were surely also at risk. The American Dream and the core of our democracy were being snatched from us, or so it seemed as many acted out their anger in the streets.

Of course, a Christian knows that our hope is not in a national mythology or our personal success but in the person of Jesus and the promised presence of God's Holy Spirit. Still, we sometimes become confused about the nature of hopefulness—as a feeling—and about where we can securely anchor our hope.

Hopeful is one of hundreds of words that emotion researchers use to describe our feelings. The work of Yale University professor Marc Brackett helps public school teachers and their students distinguish among one hundred feelings.[2] Christian counselor Aundi Kolber offers ninety-six.[3] Paul Ekman, whose work inspired the television show *Lie to Me*, aligned dozens of words describing feelings into seven clusters that register in facial expressions commonly recognized across culture—anger, contempt, disgust, enjoyment, fear, sadness, and surprise.[4]

If you compare these experts' overlapping, but still very different, constellations of feeling words, they add up to nearly two hundred words. Even more feelings appear in their writings. The words omitted from their schemas often describe feelings that can't occur in isolation; they must occur in a context. Some are feelings about social connections: *appreciated, belonging, supported, cared for, insecure, secure, compassionate, caring, respectful, respected, comforted, understood, polarized*, *vulnerable*, *embarrassed*. Some relate to tasks: *uninterested*, *pressured*, *burdened*, *overwhelmed*, *fulfilled*, *inspired*, *bored*, *indifferent*, *accomplished*.

WHY NAME OUR FEELINGS?

Having more than two hundred different words to describe feelings can seem like overkill. But there's clear value in recognizing the differences among feelings. Naming a feeling correctly helps us manage it successfully.

During the early months of COVID, many adults were helping children deal with what they called "grief" over lost opportunities: spring field trips, graduation celebrations, senior proms, first jobs. Grief is familiar to adults my age, so when I heard friends say they were helping their kids process grief over these changes, I wondered whether they were incorrectly naming as grief what might be better described as disappointment. Grief is a big feeling, and children tend to express their feelings in big ways. But if what they were seeing was not grief but oversized expressions of disappointment, then providing grief care wouldn't help. The best grief care I've experienced is a listening ear, paired with cuddles and comfort over a really long time—a year or two—with no expectation that I'll quickly pop out of my pit of sorrow. The best care I know for disappointment is a bit of cuddles and comfort, followed by large amounts of encouragement to pick a new path and a helping hand along that route. Giving grief care to someone dealing with disappointment can encourage the disappointed individual to remain stuck in a situation that might be overcome, undermining the development of ingenuity, persistence, and resilience. And, similarly, giving disappointment care to someone dealing with grief makes it far less possible to live within the pain for long enough to allow God's healing to occur.

Recognizing our feelings, understanding the information they provide, and making intentional choices about how to use them to God's glory is a long-standing part of our Christian tradition. Some classic traditions of spiritual direction urge issuing angry mental rebukes to our own difficult feelings in order to push them out of mind. They echo in some ways Paul's description of his own habit: "I strike a blow to my body and make it my slave" (1 Corinthians 9:27). Others encourage an approach more like contemporary mindfulness therapies: observe feelings as if from a distance; learn anything there is to learn from them; and don't let the feelings insist on control.[5] I find myself remembering Martin Luther's metaphorical admonition about avoiding sinful behavior: The birds of temptation—including the temptation to be overwhelmed by strong feelings—may fly overhead, but there's no need to let them nest in my hair. Successfully managing feelings requires knowing that feelings aren't less than thoughts; they're simply different from thoughts.

Without feelings, we would miss some of the information God has encoded into our systems of gathering and responding to God's world. What we call instinct or gut feeling is a form of knowledge that bypasses the intellect. People who are highly intuitive have generally learned over time that their feelings about a particular decision aren't irrational. Those feelings instead represent the outcome of a decision-making process that occurs without conscious thought. The decision that is felt or intuited can typically be validated against information they in fact have.

Feelings are more than just a decision-making tool, however. Many feelings are at the core of what allows us to connect and bond in human community. Empathy depends on our ability to gather and respond to emotional information—"feelings data" as it were—from those around us.[6] Sometimes our safety also depends on recognizing our feelings. There are times when feelings you don't want to experience are feelings you can't afford to ignore. When you feel "creeped out" in someone's presence, your feelings may be trying to help you steer clear of danger. To entirely ignore those feelings may mean putting yourself or someone in your congregation at otherwise avoidable risk. When the situation involves caregiving, even care as limited as meal drop-off after a hospital stay, it may be important to identify a different caregiver or to send caregivers in a team for safety. Feelings can be oversensitive, but they can also provide warning signals we need. Ministry teams can allow for helpful feedback, support, and handoffs in these situations.

Some have been trained to subject feelings to their intellect, even to the point of ignoring their feelings. This is its own hazard. When we ignore feelings, we can leave ourselves at risk not just from other people, but also from the feelings themselves. Feelings can control people who don't acknowledge and attribute them. Left to themselves, some feelings dissipate. Others fester. And other feelings seize control—creating sleepless nights, a racing heart, fuzzy or incoherent thoughts, among many other difficulties—in their attempt to gain your attention.

When children express very large feelings, this is usually normal. It's part of our job as adults to help them understand those feelings and wisely choose how to respond. When adults experience very large feelings, it sometimes comes in response to a very large experience—overwhelming awe as we watch a glorious sunrise, overpowering love when we meet our newborn, torrential sorrow upon the loss of a parent or partner.

But sometimes large feelings surge less predictably in adults. When children don't learn how to manage their emotions, they can carry that lack of emotional self-management into adulthood. And churches are full of very emotional children in big bodies, many of whom hold big jobs in big companies and donate big bucks to the offering plate. They provide big leadership to the congregation until they get into a big disagreement with someone they experience as a big threat to their own big ideas. At that moment, they become a big danger to God's people.

All that to say: big feelings and their big, disruptive effects are not confined to the people in our congregations who have diagnosed mental illnesses. Big emotions can drive marital conflicts. Congregational conflicts. Family disruption. Personal and professional incompetence. Even suicide.

Trauma-informed therapies operate from the understanding that seemingly random large feelings in adults may be late reverberations of feelings left to fester from earlier experiences. A feeling that was appropriately large at the time but inadequately honored is now unrestrained and an unwelcome burden. It may even conceal itself behind another feeling, so unacknowledged rage could live as depression; a poorly mourned loss as anger. It's hard to untangle these webs of emotion. That may be one reason many who experience large feelings as adults have simply learned to overlook our feelings. We may have been trained that our intellect is to govern our emotions, taking "captive every thought" (2 Corinthians 10:5), and there's some value in this. Some of our strongest emotions come from what remains of our precognitive ancestry. Immediate fight, flight, or freeze reactions kept us safe when even an instant's delay in response would put us at greater risk from the real, physical dangers we faced.

For some of us with more serious mental health problems, big feelings so often come at random that ignoring feelings is an essential skill. I've used intellect, persistence, and grit to maintain some sense of direction in the face of overwhelming sadness, anger, hopelessness, paranoia, and grandiosity. But skillfully ignoring my feelings also undermined my mental health in some ways. The biggest negative impact came from the skill I developed in ignoring my almost daily desire to die.

I have wanted to die on more than seven thousand days of my life, but I didn't discuss that with therapists during the first three decades of my care. In my layperson's understanding of mental health care, I was certain that to acknowledge my desire to die would put me in a psychiatric hospital. That is to say, I believed that systems of care were designed to keep me alive by removing me from everything that gave me a reason to live: my home, my job, my church, my friends. And the unfortunate reality is that my belief proved to be right. The first time I referenced this issue with a counselor, I was hospitalized. Within days of my return to work, my boss began suggesting I apply for jobs elsewhere; within months, I was let go.

Some years later, a therapist less anxious to protect me from difficult feelings was able to hear me out. *Why did you want to die?* she asked. *What would dying solve?* She successfully identified my terror of failed social encounters and started me on a path to building the social skills I had missed. Until I met that therapist, the only way my social anxiety could speak was by urging me to give up on life itself. I'm grateful I never followed its lead.

Hiding my suicidal thoughts kept me in my job, my church, and my community. It also kept me from obtaining help. That's not to say that all secrets should be shared with everyone. My employer is unlikely to be the right person to entrust with my marriage difficulties or mental health diagnosis. Some churches would not be good places, either. Still, needless secret-keeping undermines us. As Holocaust survivor and psychotherapist Edith Eva Eger has said, "It takes so much energy to keep the secret. Then the secret keeps you."[7] It's not always easy to choose the right persons to trust. For some, the confidentiality of a professional counselor is reassuring. Each of us needs at least a few people who can be trusted with the secrets that are binding our lives, including the feelings that seem ready to overwhelm.

Shutting our feelings away makes it impossible to obey some of God's clearest commands. No one who has denied herself the experience of rejoicing and mourning can "rejoice with those who rejoice; mourn with those who mourn" (Romans 12:15). Ignoring our feelings prevents us from reflecting the character of God that we see in our Scriptures, a God who is passionate in both attachments and repulsions, who loves us as a mother loves her nursing child (Isaiah 49:15), and who rages at us like a hurricane-driven storm surge (Psalm 88:7). During a private retreat, author Philip Yancey read through the entire Bible and found himself "unprepared for the joy and anguish—in short, the passion—of the God of the Universe." Yancey recognized in God a "Person as unique and distinctive and colorful as any person I know. . . . He feels delight and frustration and anger. . . . He weeps and moans with pain."[8] The Bible offers us a view into a way of life where strong feelings are not relegated to childhood but remain part of a healthy adult life. Even the life of our eternal God.

Yet even as God plunges deep into the feelings God created, we don't have the freedom to express our feelings at will or inconsiderately. We are not free to rage at or to overwhelm others on the basis of our desires. God promises and prescribes self-control for our lives (Proverbs 25:28; Galatians 5:23, among others).

Still, it is difficult to control what you can't understand, and part of understanding is often to give something a meaningful name. If the only name a parent has for the source of the shrill shrieks down the hall is "little crazy screaming thing," the parent is not likely to gain respite. Identifying the source as "my frustrated toddler who wants a snack" increases the odds of getting some peace and quiet.

The same goes for us as we experience our own wide range of feelings, especially those we consider difficult. Anger is a feeling. We can ask ourselves: Why has it come? What tint of anger does this burst wear? Is this a "righteous" anger, as some who are perpetually enraged like to call it, that finds its basis in God's wrath? Is this a petulant anger, grown from frustrated envy and personal desire? Is this a vengeful anger, founded in jealousy? Sad is a feeling. Why has it come? Have I lost something? Missed someone? Failed to achieve a goal? Failed to sleep enough?

Joy is also a feeling. Since it's a positive emotion, you might think there's no need to examine it. For me, the examination is essential. Because my version of bipolar disorder includes hypomanias that can involve an overwhelming sense of joy, I have to interrogate joy—so much so that at this point in my life, I hardly experience it. I recognize that I am happy when I discover that I am smiling.

IS IT A FEELING OR A SITUATION?

Some words we use for feelings are better understood as describing a situation. So *motivated* may be a feeling, but the near synonym *goal-oriented* requires a goal: the situation in which motivation happens. Many words for feelings are similarly dependent on social situations. Consider: affectionate, alienated, burdened, caring, comforted, compassionate, embarrassed, envious, included, jealous, loved, loving, polarized, pressured, respected, respectful, supported, tender, unappreciated, understood, vulnerable. There is no way to experience these feelings in isolation, and no effective way to address them without addressing the related social circumstance.

Recognizing the difference between feelings and situations is one way we help ourselves and others take appropriate responsibility when change is needed. So, for instance:

Lonely is a feeling; *isolated* is a situation we have power to change.

Secure is a feeling; *safe* and *belonging* are situations that may require difficult decisions about where and with whom we spend our time.

Alienated is a feeling; *left out* is a situation that might require rethinking our social group.

Loved is a feeling; *cared for* is a situation that generally demands not just God's care but the caring hands of God's people.

In recent years, we've tended to blur the line between feelings and situations as we seek to defuse difficult conversations by describing what "I feel" instead of offering a potentially accusatory "You did!" This does often help maintain relationships. At the same time, it can confuse our feelings with our social circumstances. Some of the words we now use as "feeling" words don't actually describe feelings at all. "I feel unseen" is shorthand for something like "I feel hurt or angry or annoyed because some person does not notice something of importance to me." "I feel exploited" describes anger, helplessness, and frustration that result from unfairness in a relationship of unequal power. Relying on feeling words to describe these situations puts us at risk of overlooking real sin and injustice.

BIG BUNCHES OF FEELINGS

It's also important to recognize that some feelings are best understood not on their own but in clusters. When we look at each of an individual's feelings in isolation, they might look like symptoms for that individual to deal with as part of a mental health care strategy. But a cluster of feelings in an individual can signal something different from what the various feelings, taken as symptoms, might suggest. And when feelings appear across clusters of people and in communities, it's even more likely that the meaning is larger than a diagnosis can explain. We've learned to interrogate clusters of cancers for possible local environmental contaminants. The same can be true of feeling clusters.

A timely example is loneliness. We often describe loneliness as a sense of isolation that an individual experiences when desired social connections are lacking. But experts in history and public health see a larger picture. They assemble multiple feelings we might associate with depression into the feeling cluster they describe as loneliness. US surgeon general Vivek Murthy notes that helplessness and hopelessness—feelings that mental health experts are prone to ascribe to depression—are also symptoms of loneliness. Murthy identifies loneliness as a top public health concern in the United States.[9] Historian Fay Bound Alberti describes loneliness as encompassing a cluster of emotions, which includes "a variable mixture of anger, resentment, shame, self-pity, sadness and jealousy."[10]

Australian community health pioneer Maxine Chaseling takes this concept a step further. She recognized loneliness as the unacknowledged root of a feeling cluster she observed among a group of retirement-age men. The feelings being named were anger, impatience, frustration, and general "grumpiness"—typical depression symptoms in males. But by recognizing this cluster of feelings as loneliness, and then further recognizing it as common to a particular population group, she was able to create an effective strategy to combat it. The community Men's Shed gave older men a place to gather for workshop projects and companionship. It successfully treated their loneliness as a social problem instead of trying to manage irritability and depression on an individual basis.[11] It has since become a national movement in Australia.

FINDING HOPE AMONG OUR FEELINGS

As Murthy notes, hopelessness can be a symptom of depression, a mental health condition that affects individuals, or of loneliness, a condition often rooted in the structures of our social relations. Theologian John Swinton even further emphasizes the hope-creating value of social relations: "Where there are friends there is hope. . . . Through the comforting presence of friends . . . impossibility gives way to possibility, hopelessness is transformed into hope, and negative self-esteem is nurtured into a more positive self-perception."[12]

Congregations are social enterprises that are intended to nurture hope. People learn to hope when we experience commitments being fulfilled. In fulfilled commitments we learn that the future is not random but may be infused with the goodwill of others. To make and fulfill promises to one another also requires us to live confidently toward the future where we will follow through. Promise-keeping is therefore "deeply connected to our ability to sustain hope," ethicist Christine Pohl observes.[13] The congregation whose relationships are characterized by consistency and integrity is a congregation where hope can grow.

At the same time, people have been able to hope in dire situations where the most obvious response would be to abandon any expectation, even of survival. How?

God tells us in Scripture, "Where there is no vision, the people perish" (Proverbs 29:18 KJV). In other words, we are, as people, wired to move toward the vision—future hope—we hold. Hope is the feeling that motivates us to action in relation to a future goal or reward. Sometimes we also use the word *hope* to describe that future. "You children are the hope of our family" is one traditional example.

TRUE HOPE OR FALSE HOPE?

The problem comes when the future hope we've chosen is not founded in reality. These are false hopes, and they can kill.

False hope works like the real thing at first. It also focuses us on the future, motivates us to act, and steels our resolve in the face of difficulties. But false hope can erode genuine hope. The Stockdale Paradox, named for US Navy Vice Admiral James Stockdale, describes this. Stockdale was a prisoner of war for more than seven years during the Vietnam conflict. Of the thousands of Americans taken prisoner during that conflict, only 591 survived until the war's end. According to Stockdale, the survivors weren't optimists. Instead, they balanced unshakable confidence in the future with unvarnished realism about their circumstances.

Detention camp optimists, on the other hand, fatally undermined hope by pegging it to specific release dates, he said. When one hoped-for release date after another came and went, the optimists and their followers lost hope. "They died of a broken heart," he told author Jim Collins.[14]

Stockdale saw in his comrades who survived the same hope that they would eventually be freed. But the survivors paired their confidence in ultimate freedom with a realistic understanding of the brutal circumstances they would have to endure over an entirely uncertain length of time.

The COVID-19 pandemic has become a crucible in which the quality of many of our own hopes have been tested. Career advancement, Pinterest-perfect homes, honor roll attainments, and athletic accomplishments—many of these hoped-for and worked-for goals have been snatched from our reach. Hopes that seemed entirely reasonable before the virus reached the United States have become impossible expectations. And we often forget how to hope when we can't see a reliable future.

The Bible describes a reliable future, but it is not always easy to see. God says that God knows God's own plans for us: "plans to prosper you and not to harm you, plans to give you hope and a future" (Jeremiah 29:11). We hear those words and imagine our own vision of a prosperous future derived from what we saw on a screen or heard from a platform. Then we rush toward the vision we have created, trusting it as our promised hope and future. When that vision is snatched away, so too is our hope. We have placed our faith in a false and deceptive hope.

God warns us that we see imperfectly and only in part, "through a glass, darkly" (1 Corinthians 13:12 KJV). So God offers a strategy for moving forward in uncertainty. We are to watch where the light of the Word illuminates safe footing for the next step and to advance only as far as that light allows us to see (Psalm 119:105).

Walking into what God has illuminated for me rarely takes me toward any of those grand, outward-focused visions that I so easily choose for myself. In the twenty-first-century West, we are so used to big stories about big achievements that it is easy for us to "despise the day of small things" (Zechariah 4:10). But the various restrictions of pandemic times have afforded us many opportunities to value things we might have overlooked in easier days. We discovered the slow satisfaction of starting a garden from seed; the casual pleasure of tossing a ball with the kids; the quiet self-nurturance of cooking our own healthy meals. And as we learned to value these smaller things, we also began to notice seemingly small opportunities to share kindness, warmth, and love with those around us whose hope was waning. In times when large opportunities seemed to be lacking, God gave us the opportunity to "do small things with great love," as Mother Teresa said. This time of small beginnings might build us together with many others into a home where God's Spirit dwells (Ephesians 2:22).

We live successfully with our many difficulties not by practicing the potentially false hope that they will vanish but by allowing ourselves to learn hope while in difficulty. As God tells us, "suffering produces perseverance; perseverance, character; and character, hope" (Romans 5:3-4). To learn hope from suffering isn't a lesson plan most would choose. Still, it's the course of study God provides. We can choose perseverance, character, and the real hope God gives, or allow ourselves to sink in despair under the weight of false hopes and false promises. At a time when suicide and overdose "deaths of despair" have become prominent features of US culture, God's people can show others how to choose true hope and life.

FINDING HOPE AMONG GOD'S PEOPLE

Knowing that I am fully accepted by God has been essential to my survival as a person with a bipolar diagnosis. I screw up regularly. God forgives me every time. I fall down regularly. God picks me up every time.

This is the character of relationship we're called to offer one another as part of God's body here on earth. We are able to advance in hope as we find quality friendships among the people of God, the experience of forgiveness and expectation that we will forgive, opportunities to serve others, and a place of belonging where truth-telling is the norm.

The greatest hope is often found from other people who are further along the same difficult path. Jerome Groopman, a hematologist and oncologist, describes a patient he couldn't convince to continue treatment: he learned that the man's imagination was stuck in his memories of a close friend who had died from the same condition. After a nurse allowed the patient to "accidentally" encounter another patient who was becoming healthier, the man found his vision of hope.[15]

Over the eight years I taught the Family to Family education program for the National Alliance on Mental Illness (NAMI), the session that built the most hope for many students was the class near the end when they got to meet a mental health services "consumer." I would introduce myself. Discovering that the teacher they had come to trust—a competent person with a career, a home, and a marriage—was a person with a diagnosis, just like their relative, created a hopeful vision they hadn't yet found.

This is the foundation of all recovery-based mental health programs, including Fresh Hope (previously mentioned in chapter 4), which was developed by a pastor who lives with a bipolar diagnosis. Fresh Hope provides space for those who are challenged by mental health problems to learn from those who are living more successfully with their mental health problems. Being face-to-face with people who are honest about their struggles and their advances provides the hope that your own struggles may not preclude advances. You may, in fact, have a future. And that's grounds for hope.

Hope is also nurtured when we find ourselves powerful enough to influence our own lives. Psychologist C. Richard Snyder described hope as a kind of goal-directed thought involving confidence in one's own ability to identify paths toward the goal and to take effective actions to both reach and sustain it.[16] We believe we have a worthwhile future because our experiences teach us that we can help create that kind of future.

Truth-telling is another way to build hope. Pediatric epidemiologist W. Thomas Boyce found that the children who were healthiest after the 1989 Loma Prieta earthquake in California were the children whose drawings of the earthquake were the most bleak. "The telling of fearful tales and experiences, whether in language or in art, is a human proclivity with an ancient past," he writes. "There must have been not just comfort but protection in the telling."[17]

Because true hope faces reality and also remains confident in the future, we as congregations need to reorient ourselves to painful truths while retaining our confidence that God holds our future. Many of us have returned to the biblical tradition of lament in recent years from our desire to reroot ourselves in true hope, not just a wished-for way of life. "Those who hope in God can no longer put up with reality as it is, but begin to suffer under it, to contradict it," says the Rev. William J. Barber II.[18] We need to lament the lies our culture lives by: that achievements measure merit, that dollars earned represent the value of a person, that those with darker skin tones are worthy of suspicion, that those who bear children are less worthy of their wages.

We begin to find true hope when we agree with God that our hope has been built on many things that are considerably less than Jesus' blood and righteousness (to paraphrase the old hymn). Some of what we hope in may even carry us away from what God aims to do in and through us. To connect with the hope God has for us requires us to tell the truth about our false hopes so we can turn from their dangers.

SMALL BEGINNINGS: NAME IT AND FRAME IT

God experiences feelings, and as beings made in God's image, we are designed to experience them as well. When we name our feelings, we begin to understand them and, through that process, ourselves. From that more stable space, we are in a better position to assess and assemble our own next step toward hope.

Psychologist Everett Worthington uses a metaphor from homebuilding. To make a support pillar, you don't pour concrete on the ground. You pour concrete into wooden forms, which have been constructed to hold the concrete in place and in the right shape until it solidifies.[19] The concrete represents the work of God, which over time solidifies in our life; the forms represent the work we do to make the right kind of space for God.

This work can be done both by ourselves and by others. One of the forms that built hope in my life was a simple lesson in social skills from an ordinary layperson. I always found it daunting to enter a room full of people. Who could I talk with? I had plenty of experience trying to enter conversational groups only to find myself at someone's back. Brent, a Methodist layman and technology marketer, told our chamber of commerce meeting how to read social groups so we could join in successfully. I tried his trick at the next event, and it worked. Instead of teaching me to manage my social anxiety with breathing exercises or thought corrections, Brent taught me how to avoid social anxiety in what had been a difficult setting for me. Many times, our feelings are best managed by learning new skills that an ordinary layperson, like Brent, can easily teach. And when we find ourselves powerful to conquer a life challenge, this builds hope.

THE CHALLENGE

Feelings are powerful because they're designed to be. The most primal of our feelings are designed to bond us to others—because the group can be a source of safety—and to quickly remove us from danger. Trying to shut down or ignore these feelings puts us at risk. But allowing them to run our life creates its own risks.

Many of us have been taught to rely on our intellect instead of our emotions, and that lesson is valuable as far as it goes. It encourages us to step back from those powerful primal responses and ask questions like, Is my feeling bigger than this situation requires? Does my feeling provide any useful information? Is there more than one way to respond to the information this feeling exposes?

We get into trouble when we try to substitute intellect for emotion. The God who made us in the image of our Creator shows a remarkable range of powerful emotion in the Bible, which suggests that we, like God, should expect to experience a range of powerful emotions. Those emotions hold value.

Yet it can be difficult for others to recognize the perfectly ordinary person inside the extraordinary display, the over-whelming expression, the overwhelmed life. It is hard to encourage the virtue of temperance—moderation—while acknowledging the valuable experiences of transcendence and sorrow that drive us. It is equally difficult to encourage the virtues and skills of social relations in a person whose own feelings seem like challenge enough.

For an individual with mental health problems, the special challenge is to discern the useful feelings—those that come in response to a situation and give clues to personal values and purpose—from the feelings that simply come like storm surges. There is rarely any meaning to be found in the latter.

All that can be done is to set the feeling aside and do the next thing. But without good discernment, a person risks either ignoring big feelings that have useful information or attending excessively to feelings whose only meaning is to show that one's body is out of whack right now.

And where, within all those feelings, does hope live?

On one level, it's really open to question whether hope is a personal feeling at all. Like love, hope exists only in a context. We experience love in the context of relationships. Hope is what we experience when we have a vision for the future.

But life forecloses many visions for many people. The choice to care for a family forecloses professional goals for many— whether because they are at-home parents or because they are providing from an unsatisfying job. The choice to pursue a career in a distant city forecloses in some measure the vision of close relations with aging parents. Living with a disability or a serious mental health problem constrains life options in ways many consider limiting.

When living in times and places that foreclose our visions for our current life in this world, many of us can choose no vision other than God. All we know is that one day, we will see God face-to-face in that city where the trees always bear good, ripe fruit.

Some hope in chariots. Some in horses. Some in career progress or grandchildren. We are called to hope in what God promises to those who belong to the family of God.

THE GOOD NEWS
The good news for those who feel hopeless is simple.

Hope *is*.

There's an extraordinarily long history of people who live with suffering and bear up because we know that hope *is*. We may not experience the feeling of hope, but we hear about it from others. We read about it in Scripture. We trust that God ensures it.

Mental health recovery experts, even those working in entirely secular contexts, urge us to help those experiencing mental health problems identify sources of hope that are meaningful to them. The US Substance Abuse and Mental Health Services Administration puts it this way: "Hope, the belief that these challenges and conditions can be overcome, is the foundation of recovery."[20]

Hope is not so much a feeling as a belief. It's a belief that there is a future, and that the future can be better. And as we learned from those imprisoned during wars, the hope that sustains must have its foundation in truth. To rely on a hope that can prove fickle or false is to lean on nothing helpful at all. We serve each other well when we nurture confidence that together we can recognize true hope.

For those deepest in a pit, true hope might be as small as "If I hold my cat, he will purr." It could be as close in time as "Tomorrow, when the store opens, I can buy bread and make toast." It could be today's tiny seed of the barely dared dream: "I want to write a book, so today I will write a sentence." When people live in days of very small beginnings, we are called to rejoice (see Zechariah 4:6-10).

Beginning to hope is the work of our Lord. Hope is, now and forever, for all of us.

8

The Competent Caregiver's Toolkit: Humility

Humility is the virtue by which we see the truth.
—**VASSILIOS PAPAVASSILIOU**, *Thirty Steps to Heaven*

Pete Costas was still relatively young in his career as a Salvation Army officer the Sunday evening that a fidgety, distracted, and somewhat disheveled young man walked in well after the service had started and seated himself at the center of the front row. Captain Costas was just beginning his message when the man's hand shot up in the air. He had a question.

Captain Costas answered it and returned to his message. A few sentences later, the hand shot up again.

This time, after answering the question, Captain Costas asked a favor. He pointed out the other people in the room and asked the young man if he thought he could hold his questions until the end so the others could hear the rest of the message.

Afterward, the captain said, the two of them could go together to his office and he'd answer all the man's questions.

The young man nodded his agreement and quickly sat on his hands.

After the service, the young man joined Costas in his office and rapid-fired questions at him about God, salvation, and what it meant to be in relationship with Jesus. Costas referenced John 3:16 in his answer.

As Costas tells the story, the young man's face went blank for a second and then he said, "Can you say that again? They told me to ask you to say that again."

Costas asked, "Who told you to ask me that?"

The young man answered calmly: "I didn't want to tell you this, but I have sort of like a mind meld with aliens. They can see you through my eyes and hear you through my ears, but they can't communicate with you directly. They told me to ask you to say that again."

Costas repeated John 3:16: "For God so loved the world that He gave His only begotten Son, that whoever believes in Him should not perish but have everlasting life " (NKJV).

The young man pushed on. "Now this Jesus," he asked, "died for the sins of the world?"

"Yes," the captain replied.

"They want to know if he died for the sins of the universe," he said.

That was a new one. Costas thought for a minute.

"Well," he reasoned, "if God created the heavens and the earth, and Jesus is his only begotten Son, and Jesus died once for the sins of all, then yes, he died for the sins of the universe."

"That's exactly what they wanted to hear!" the young man exclaimed. And he got up and, with a spring in his step, walked out.[1]

Just as missionaries approach new cultures with humility and love, so we too must approach those whose minds carry them to places unfamiliar to us. They may be an older adult with dementia. They may be a friend with a psychotic disorder. They may be a new acquaintance who has passed through unimaginable fires of war and dislocation. The competent caregiver walks humbly with a sufferer where that person goes, trusting that as we go in and go out, God will keep all of us safe (John 10:9-10).

When we take our turn giving supportive care to those who suffer from cancer or a traumatic brain injury, we don't concern ourselves with diagnoses or treatment strategies. Those are the province of medical professionals, and we readily admit them outside our expertise. We concern ourselves, instead, with the person who is suffering. We attend to her anxiety about the diagnosis or lack of diagnosis. We listen empathetically to the patient who may be prepared to battle the illness or ready to let it take him down. We comfort the family, which may be shredded by disagreements over care strategies. We walk humbly into our caregiving responsibilities, knowing that our expertise is limited and our God's love infinite.

THE HIDDEN VIRTUE OF HUMILITY

Humility is a traditional virtue that can be hard to understand in the twenty-first century. It describes a willingness to follow, not lead; to do good unnoticed instead of expecting honors. Dictionary definitions sometimes describe it as a state of low self-worth, which is not at all accurate. Humility is more correctly a state of accurate self-assessment, as the apostle Paul prescribes in Romans 12:3-8. In accordance with God's guidance, humility values the self, but no more highly than it values others. It is as happy applauding as being applauded, being dependent as being depended upon. Humility is the condition wherein all our humanness and human experience are recognized as poor imitations of our good God, but are still valued for the glimpse they offer us of God's character and purposes in the Creator's world.

US culture obscures humility with our belief in earned achievement and opportunity. We describe ourselves—not very accurately—as a meritocracy, a place where rewards consistently flow in direct proportion to talent and hard work. Thomas Jefferson described the fledgling country as based on a "natural Aristocracy among men . . . [grounded in] virtue and talents,"[2] where advancement depended not on ancestry but personal achievement. The poor but plucky heroes of Horatio Alger's popular fiction a century later fit the mold: these young men overcome their challenging beginnings through diligence, optimism, and integrity (although a wealthy benefactor often plays a role as well). The word *meritocracy* would not be coined until nearly two centuries into our national life. It describes a way of life that has never been fully true in this country, but is central to how we think about life in the United States.

In a perfect meritocracy, winners deserve their successes because of their greater merits, and losers deserve to fail. As meritocracy plays out in the United States today, notes Harvard political philosopher Michael Sandel, winners develop the excessive pride of hubris, as they feel responsibility for their achievements. Losers are humiliated, as they believe that they are personally responsible for their failures, even when vaguely aware that outcomes are significantly shaped by circumstances of birth and heritage they did not control.[3] In a meritocracy, we are not just humbled by our limits; we are humiliated to discover ourselves limited.

Failing to acknowledge ourselves as limited is, of course, the sin Satan encouraged in the garden of Eden. "You will be like God," he hissed (Genesis 3:5), and our first parents were all too willing to go along. The idea that some things might just be beyond the limits of our own created bodies, minds, or competencies is not easy for us to accept. Nor do we readily acknowledge the possibility that some of the good we enjoy might have come from a place beyond our personal strivings. The United States, for example, is among the world cultures where life opportunities are highly determined by family of origin. A child born to a low-income family in the United States is less likely to advance to a higher status than a child similarly born in most of Europe and developing Asia.[4] The evidence doesn't support our belief that lifetime achievement is based on individual merit. Meritocracy is a new idea that just isn't proving out.

To be able to live in humility requires recognizing that what one is and has are all gifts from God—including the talent and energy that make greater achievement possible for some. Humility can lead to an upside-down understanding of 1 Corinthians 12: If those least worthy of honor are clothed with greatest honor, then the considerable talents with which God gifted me may simply represent God's best effort to make sure the body will find in me something of value. In my own case, that would make those gifts (at least in part) generous accommodation for the limitations placed on me by my mental health problems.

HOW HUMILITY SHAPES MENTAL HEALTH MINISTRIES

Humility is a core virtue in our mental health ministries. To look on self and others with humility requires us to look past the standards that demonstrate merit in one particular culture, and to look at whether we are as God asks us to be. It requires the kind of humility that missionaries ideally bring to their cross-cultural communications of good news, when they acknowledge that they have arrived but must learn to understand the place where they've landed.

Missionaries know that to make the good news understood, they have to translate not just its words but its concepts. Carol and Don Richardson learned this when their early gospel sharing among the Sawi of New Guinea drew cheers for Judas because he so perfectly embodied the cultural values of treachery and deception. Happily, the missionaries were humble enough to continue studying the culture and discover what they would eventually describe as the "redemptive analogy" at its heart: the idea that groups at war could exchange a "peace child" to end the dispute and ensure future stability. That Sawi practice helped them reposition Jesus in the minds of their listeners. He was no longer the dupe of Judas, but the "peace child" sent by a great leader.[5]

To practice humility when we encounter differences requires us to abandon both fear and pride. The person who is afraid of another can't listen well or extend a gracious welcome. Those who look at the other from their own prideful sense of self are not able to learn in any meaningful way. When we are friends to those whose mental health conditions differ from our own, we have to be willing to not understand: why they don't want to go for a walk on a lovely day, why they didn't return the call, why they believe that they caused it to rain by going outside to smoke. It's okay to not understand, even when we want desperately to understand well enough to plunge in and fix whatever's wrong. Repair may not be our responsibility as we walk alongside people, with God, on their long mental health journey.

When we think about mental health problems in the twenty-first-century West, we tend to think about ways to fix them quickly. We refer people to psychiatrists and general practitioners for medications. To counselors for a round of evidence-based cognitive behavioral therapy. We offer groups in the church and beyond—DivorceCare, GriefShare, and more—to provide facilitated support services that fit readily into our Sunday school or life group's twelve-week quarters. We expect mental health problems to be as readily overcome as one of the illnesses for which antibiotics proved a twentieth-century miracle cure.

The reality is that any course of professional treatment, even one that uses medications, typically requires more than a few weeks to resolve a mental health problem. But if two weeks is the longest a person should tolerate emotional distress before being diagnosed, then why would a person tolerate a treatment program that requires an extended period of effort? And why should a person tolerate the long, difficult road that walking with *someone else* in distress may require?

Even a small mental health problem makes life more challenging, both for the person with the problem and for the people around the individual. There will be times when the depressed person doesn't pull equal weight in the household, workplace, church, or community. The person in mania or even hypomania doesn't let anyone else get a word in and may blast through the family savings in a matter of weeks. The person suffering from paranoia may stay awake for days on end and damage all the locks in the house by constantly testing them. Those who have not lived with a person who suffers a severe mental health problem generally don't understand just how difficult this can be. We're prone to look for explanations in the hope that we'll find the right place to push and, *presto!* The hidden door will pop open and reveal the remedy.

Unfortunately, efforts to dive into explanations rapidly drag us into waters that are far too deep for nonprofessionals. Those who aren't trained counselors or medical doctors are better equipped for compassionate care than for remediation. Still, it's tough to wait for lessons to take root, skills to be learned, and God to work in the difficult behaviors and attitudes of those around us. Our impatient culture teaches us that we deserve better than whatever we have and whoever surrounds us, and we deserve better *now*.

In the same way that treating biological issues is often beyond many of us, so are the challenges related to traumatic experiences. Many books have been written on the role that trauma plays in creating mental health problems. The range of traumatic experiences people can encounter in this life is remarkable. The impact of those experiences can be unpredictable. In much of the world, trauma inflicted by war, genocide, starvation, forced relocation, and sexual assault is an unfortunate norm. In the more secure North American setting, some communities still live with disproportionate trauma from ongoing discrimination, daily microaggressions, dangerous surroundings, and lack of essentials. Even among the more fortunate, seemingly small encounters can inflict oversized trauma that resounds for years after, in forms that may go unrecognized as trauma impact. Almost anyone's life can be affected by interpersonal trauma.

People lock up traumatic experiences for lots of reasons. Often, it's as simple as the need to keep going. Our lives may not afford us space and time to be completely shut down, so we allow ourselves to live as best we can with whatever limits they pose. This leads to one of the core affirmations of trauma-informed caregiving: people are all doing the best they can.[6]

We also lock up our traumatic experiences because revisiting them is so painful—sometimes painful enough to be disabling. The remembering of traumatic experiences can't be done helpfully with a counselor unskilled in transitioning people past their trauma. Simply reliving the trauma carries a person back into dark places without providing an escape route.

Several Christian ministries have carried faith-based trauma healing frameworks into countries where trauma is more overt than in the United States. Most widely used is the study guide *Healing the Wounds of Trauma: How the Church Can Help*, which has been translated into more than 150 languages over nearly two decades of use. This simplified language curriculum was initially developed for countries racked by war, famine, weather catastrophes, rapes of conquest, and epidemics of HIV/AIDS. The North American edition also addresses suicide, domestic abuse, and addiction. Since 2004, this resource from the Trauma Healing Institute has established a track record of effective care by Christian laypeople in countries where access to medical psychiatry and professional counseling is severely limited.

THE HUMILITY OF ACCEPTING OUR LIMITS

It's frustrating to want to fix something and not know how. All these experiences of not yet understanding, not yet being able to remedy, not yet even being able to discuss what has harmed us force us to confront our limits as people and caregivers. In this, we can learn a great deal from those who live with what we more readily recognize to be limiting conditions. I work with adults who have intellectual disabilities. People don't find it difficult to understand that these adults may not found a large company or invent the next technological breakthrough.[7] We also are happy to enjoy the ways they bring value to our world. The organization I work for runs art studio programs that are nationally recognized for affording our clients the opportunity to express themselves creatively in artworks that sell readily, including to collectors.

Living with limits is living in the world as it is, not the world that our ambitions and our social media feeds cause us to imagine. To walk with humility requires us to recognize that all the good we have—even the good we feel we have earned—is a gift from God. And that the limits others experience are not causes for blame, but something to view with compassion and to be supported as "weak knees" that deserve steadying (Isaiah 35:3; Hebrews 12:12).

Mental health problems do pose limits, both to those of us who experience them directly and to those who must live with and around us. Stanley Hauerwas describes our created lives as "a story we have not chosen."[8] The more seriously limiting our life conditions, the less likely we would choose the life we face. And when we live in "a hope schooled by medicine," the more we want to believe in easy pharmaceutical fixes that will eliminate limits and the suffering they cause. We try to rewrite the story God gave us into a different story we prefer. Then, when difficulties continue despite our best efforts, "it challenges our most precious and profound belief that humanity has in fact become god."[9]

The unfortunate paradox is that as we pridefully reimagine medical science as savior, we push it far from the humble work of good scientists.

A HUMBLE SCIENCE OF MENTAL HEALTH

Good science lives in the humble space between the wonder of the question and the wonder of discovery. There is no more lovely quest for solid, measurable, useful human knowledge.

But good scientists today often find themselves caught in a noisy space between the joy of discovery and the aggressive marketing of contemporary research. Today a scientist must sell research plans to funders. Funders may not direct the research, but they can decide whether the outcomes may be published to inform other scientists and the public.

The sheer hucksterism of sales-driven science has filled my media streams for years. In my lifetime, butter has been unhealthier than margarine because of its cholesterol content, then healthier because it lacked artificial ingredients. Unhealthy salt was removed from thousands of products, then lavishly sprinkled in large grains on others. Coffee was a hazard, then a productivity aid. Chocolate was a high-calorie enemy, then a high-antioxidant boost.

Of course, I knew better than to even *consider* bad reports about chocolate.

The science behind current mental health strategies is likewise in process. Guidance changes as the evidence base evolves. In my lifetime, benzodiazepines have progressed from helpful antianxiety medicine to dangerous addictive drugs to widely prescribed medicines once again. They are no longer described as causing addiction, but are characterized as just having the potential for creating physical dependence.[10] Treatments change as the evidence base changes, and treatments can also lag far behind the available scientific evidence base, in part because it takes time to train practitioners in new strategies. So, for example, the impact of trauma on mental health is well established, but helpful trauma-informed treatments are less widely available than biomedical approaches. In the meantime, it is still common among laypeople and some practitioners to describe depression as the result of chemical deficiencies in the brain and to focus on various serotonin-modifying medications, even though science has concluded, in its usual humble phrasing, that after several decades of research the serotonin hypothesis about depression "has not been clearly substantiated."[11] Anglican priest Kathryn Greene-McCreight says it more plainly: "The biological model, strictly understood, does not hold water even among psychiatrists and research scientists."[12]

Given the humble nature of good science, it behooves all of us to view the scientific information we are given about mental health with humility as well. Christian people have cared for those with mental health problems for as long as we have been followers of Jesus. All of us are bound to feel uncertain about current science from time to time, whether because we are not scientists ourselves or because we are humble scientists who recognize that scientific discovery never ends.

SMALL BEGINNINGS: GIVE UP EXPECTATIONS

Humility lives in the uncomfortable place of accepting what is. It helps us understand that both God and medicine may work miracles of dramatic healing, and also to know that God decides when and whether that happens. Diligent works of prayer, Scripture study, fasting, service, and worship music carry their own value in the kingdom, but they aren't currency to be exchanged for a better life in this world. Humility allows God to do the work and get the credit while we continue the long journey alongside our more challenged and less challenged friends.

THE CHALLENGE

It's not easy to walk humbly into the persistent difficulties that long-term mental health challenges can pose. To encounter someone's mental health challenges with humility is to first admit that you're entering a strange land where the terrain is unmapped and the rules you know as normal don't apply. It requires us to accept the possibility that we may be unable to fix or even significantly improve the difficult circumstances a dearly loved other endures. To live with your own challenges requires a different kind of humility: the humility of continuing to walk into the larger human community despite being often—or even usually—misunderstood and undervalued.

In our present culture, pride rules. Scientific research proves it: Those who gain high place in business and industry are more likely than others to practice and rationalize a wide range of sins—especially pride, deceit, and self-centeredness.[13] Unfortunately, the manifold reckonings of recent years remind us that these sins run through religious institutions as well. As God's people, we have been living in the world—as we are called to do—and too often we have unfortunately become people of the world. To choose humility feels like a frightening loss of control. And in many ways it is. To live humbly in a world ruled by pride is to acknowledge that you are unlikely to join its rulers. The meek only inherit the earth; the proud control it now.

While humility requires giving up control, it also offers genuine security. Humility allows us to acknowledge the end of our own control and the completeness of God's rule. It reflects an accurate self-assessment. And this truth sets us free indeed.

Practicing humility in the face of someone else's mental health challenges is difficult. We may face some anxiety as we recognize: I don't understand what's going on here. I could make things worse. Things could get very difficult for me. Then we recognize: Things could get worse with or without my help. Or they might never change. Or they could get better.

I used to talk regularly with a man who was often unable to distinguish reality from the creations of his own mind. The conversations frustrated and overwhelmed me. I would turn afterward to a mutual friend and sputter about how impossible the man was. My friend would remind me that frustration was an ordinary response to unreal beliefs, and that neither the frustration nor the beliefs were likely to change soon. Within a week or two the tables would turn, and I'd be issuing the same reminder to my friend. To humble ourselves enough to simply be present and listen did not come easily to either of us.

Practicing humility in your own mental health challenges is also difficult. Life with a mental health problem is full of humiliations large and small. To the extent you are able to conceal your struggles, you are treated like any other person. To the extent that you disclose, you generally lose the right to be fully human. If a person with a known diagnosis is fatigued and takes time out, people think her depression is acting up. If he's wronged and becomes angry, his anger is dismissed as mania. Even when you live closeted, the differences between you and everyone else eventually emerge, to your profound embarrassment. I think of two kind senior professional women at a church I once attended who took on the task of coaching me to improve my work performance. In our second early-morning coffee meeting, my description of a workplace situation startled them. I caught their surprised glances at each other before one of them asked carefully, "And what caused you to think that would be an appropriate reaction?"

Well, the short answer would be, I didn't know better. Even though I was, at the time, nearly fifty years old. And unfortunately for my personal growth, the humiliation of that moment led me to cancel any future meetings. I was not yet humble enough to accept that I was a senior professional with the social skills of a tenth grader.

THE GOOD NEWS

Humility isn't a popular lesson plan in the twenty-first century. But the lessons of humble listening and release of control we take from our interactions with those who are suffering mental health problems are lessons we can carry into our other relationships as well.

When a person diagnosed with Alzheimer's asks me for the third time today whether my brother gave me a ride, I know to smile and answer again, "Yes! He's so helpful!" When a person caught in paranoid delusions announces for the third time today, "That crooked cop is trying to steal my house," I know to frown and answer again, "Wow. That must be so upsetting." Neither person's disordered thoughts are likely to become like my own soon. All I can do is walk humbly with these people in the world where they currently live, trusting that God comes with me into their world just as Jesus came humbly into this world where we live.

Humbly walking into these uncharted terrains requires releasing ourselves from many of the kinds of measurable outcomes we imagine. At the same time, it allows us the delight of seeing God accomplish outcomes we might never have expected. One chaplain to an Alzheimer's care facility says that the staff reports better moods and calmer behavior for the rest of the day after each of his visits. When Captain Costas began listening to the young man who said he had "a kind of mind meld with aliens," could Costas have imagined that he would release the young man from fear for those imaginary aliens' souls?

God spoke truly when God told us that in this life we would experiences tests and temptation and pain, that we would be liberated only when we attain the new heaven and earth. There, the tears that have watered our lives will cease to exist, and our sorrows and suffering will vanish.

Having what we call a mental illness is a challenge. Living faithfully among people with mental health problems is a challenge. But God is able. With God's power and our own insufficiency, we must be content . . . and humbled.

9

The Competent Caregiver's Toolkit: Fearlessness

All great and beautiful work has come of first gazing without shrinking into the darkness.

—**JOHN RUSKIN**, "The Lance of Pallas," in *Modern Painters*, vol. 5

Who isn't afraid sometimes of things that are different or unpredictable? And since people with mental health problems can often be different or unpredictable, what reasonable person wouldn't be afraid of them?

To be afraid of what seems beyond our control is normal. It's hardwired, even instinctual, to be cautious of those who are "outside of my tribe." Who could seem further from my safe, familiar community of friends than someone who almost never musters a smile? Someone who this week throws ideas into the world like Mardi Gras beads and another week won't even watch the parades from the balcony? Part of what makes it possible to trust a person is to be able to anticipate what that person is likely to do. We don't trust certain people because they've left us hanging in the past or even actively injured us. They aren't safe. We're afraid of them.

And yet God tells us, "Be not afraid." Over and over. It's just not reasonable.

Fear has accompanied our mental health conversation for decades. Films presented mentally ill characters to frighten us almost as soon as silent movies were made.[1] After large state psychiatric hospitals closed in the 1960s, the figures we'd learned to fear moved from asylums to alleys. People with serious mental illnesses became at first the homeless folk we saw muttering on street corners, then the dangerous people described in the media. A study of mental health reporting in major US media over two decades (1995–2014) found that more than half of all the stories described violent behavior by people with diagnoses[2]; fewer than one in six described people successfully treated for or recovered from mental illness.[3]

Who wouldn't be afraid to encounter people widely described as violent and uncurable?

Of course, if your congregation looks at all like the rest of our nation, then one in every six people of all ages is currently taking medication to treat a diagnosed mental health condition. That means there is probably someone who takes psychiatric medication sitting in every single row.

Does that make you afraid? Why not?

Are they afraid to tell you? Why?

Does their own life frighten them? How?

In the next pages, I'm going to encourage you to consider the fears we all face as we encounter mental health problems in ourselves and others. Then we'll consider ways we can similarly face our fears to live successfully as part of a body that includes people with mental health challenges.

OUR FEARS ABOUT MENTAL HEALTH PROBLEMS

Fear drives much of our thinking about mental health problems and how we respond to them. We often fear that someone may suffer as a result of mental health problems:

- Someone—especially if it's me or my own child—will miss out on life experiences that those without mental health problems enjoy.
- Someone with mental health problems may become violent against me or others.
- Someone with mental health problems will ask too much of me or become dependent on me.
- Someone with mental health problems will die by suicide and I'll blame myself for not having helped enough.

Our systems of care and social stigmas create other fears for those who live with mental health problems. My friends and I live with fears like these:

- The prescribed medicines won't work.
- The prescribed medicines will damage competencies that matter to me—my ability to find my way home from the store, play the piano, or locate the next word in the sentence I'm speaking, for example.
- The prescribed medicines will damage my health, perhaps injuring my kidneys, launching a prediabetic metabolic syndrome, or making me addicted.[4]
- Someone will find out I'm treated for a mental health problem, and I'll lose my job or be shut out from meaningful ministry.
- Someone will overreact to my extravagant expressions of my feelings, and I'll be ostracized.

- The medicines will make me suicidal, and I'll be hospitalized.[5]

All of those fears combine in the unfortunately realistic fears that mental health problems could cause people to lose their income. Or their family. Or their dignity. Or their place of respect and responsibility in church and community.

I recall one family where the dad was a successful professional, the mom was at home with three kids, and both were leaders in their church. They kept the mom's bipolar disorder secret because she valued her role as head of the Sunday school. She didn't believe anyone would trust her with their children if they knew about her diagnosis, even though medical treatment was effectively managing her condition.

When baby number four came, the church stepped up with the usual parade of new baby dinners. They had no idea that Dad was managing not just his job, three preschoolers, and a new baby, but a mommy who had flown into a postpartum mania. Fear of what could happen if they shared this reality trapped the family in isolation as they faced an unusually difficult situation.

Those of us dealing with mental health problems cannot rely on our minds to help us manage these fears, either. A person who lives with a bodily disability can rely on their mind to make sense of their challenges and to assist in stabilizing their entirely understandable emotional reactions. The mind challenged with mental health problems is less helpful. What others rely on, we're struggling to rein in while trying to locate any piece of ourselves that might pull the reins. At its worst, this can be paralyzing. With the right supports, it is possible—but by no means guaranteed—that we may become more effective in living with the challenges our lives pose.

LIVING FEARLESSLY WITH MENTAL HEALTH PROBLEMS

At the same time, mental health problems can engender a measure of fearlessness that looks very much like the way of life that God calls us to. My mental health problems often make me fearless where others might feel anxious:

Less afraid of differences. You see me as awkward during a Bible study or at coffee hour when I fail to behave as the middle-class American Christian that I am. And because I find it difficult to navigate these ordinary circumstances, I don't find it more difficult to address situations that involve greater differences.

I once worked with a brilliant computer whiz who was a first-generation immigrant. When he answered my question about his accent with a hard-edged "I grew up in the *jungles* of Barbados," I didn't think twice before responding, "But there *are* no jungles in Barbados." We had many conversations after that about his experiences of American racism, including being detained and spread-eagled by police as he walked from the university library back to his apartment late one night.

When you aren't afraid of people who are different, you can engage with people that others overlook. When marginalized people can see that you're different from others, they recognize that in being different, you are like them. You can see opportunities to be God's hands and feet in service because you notice people who are—like yourself—unable to hide the reality that they live in need.

Less afraid to be different. I don't have much choice about being different. No matter how carefully I try to mimic your behavior, your wardrobe, your activities, your interests, I know by experience that there will be a moment when my differences are publicly exposed. Perhaps the Bible study leader will ask a question that hits a tender spot. A few group members will dab their eyes. My tears will gush nonstop. Others, whether weepy or not, will turn their heads. I'll be shut out of the end-of-evening goodbyes.

Knowing that most people—Christian or not—see me as different means I'm accustomed to being different. If my understanding of biblical norms places me outside the American cultural norm, I can live with that. If my understanding of biblical norms places me outside the American *Christian* norm, I can live with that, too. I am forced by my mental health problems to acknowledge that I am who I am because I am largely without the option of molding myself into whatever is currently acceptable.[6]

Less anxious in high-risk settings. I'm not very good at reading social cues, and other people often find my reactions inappropriate, if not totally confounding. That means there are very few social settings where I feel secure. For many years, almost every interaction felt risky, which made me paradoxically more willing to take some kinds of risks: whether engaging a stranger in conversation about God or offering prayer to a business colleague in distress. When very little feels safe, then very few new settings feel relatively dangerous. I reserve my greatest anxiety for situations that remind me of settings where I've failed in the past—which are, of course, many. Still, because I cannot trust myself, I must try to trust God. That's a good thing.

Less afraid of death. Like many people with chronic health diagnoses, I've been told that my life expectancy is limited. We used to hear that one in four people with bipolar dies by suicide, often in their thirties. So when I hit forty, I had truly conquered a hill on which many die. It's still common to say that people treated for serious mental illnesses die, on average, twenty-five years earlier than the general population. That would mean that at age sixty-three, I've beaten the odds again.[7] When you live with death front of mind, you have to choose fear or choose life. For four decades, I've chosen life.

More resilient. Bipolar disorder is an illness that can destroy careers and relationships. At its least damaging, it tends to create a person who runs in shame—over and over—from the embarrassments she has created. People with bipolar start over again and again and again.

Paradoxically, one word to describe this behavior is a positive one: resilience. Resilience describes how people who have experienced adversity bounce back. We often focus on ways to build resiliency in early childhood for a successful adult life. For me, resilience is a skill learned as an adult. When I experience a disaster or create a disaster, I have learned simply to stand—again. Many people have skills that keep them from falling. I have exceptional skill at getting off the floor. God calls this "perseverance" and reminds us that God provides what we need so that after we have done all we can do ourselves, we will stand (Ephesians 6:13).

LIVING FEARLESSLY AMONG PEOPLE WHO ARE DIFFERENT
Jesus said that it was only by becoming like little children that we could walk with him into the reign of God (Matthew 18:3; Mark 10:15; Luke 18:17). One of the ways infants differ from adults is that they actually prefer unusual behavior to outcomes that are easily predicted.[8] Perhaps this is a way we can become community to those with mental health problems: by again welcoming our childlike interest in what is different. As long as we continue to seek safety in communities of sameness, we miss God's call to live with love and compassion in the community of all God's children.

Some of the reasons we fear people with mental health challenges are bound up in our mythologies. We fear they will violently harm us, for example, when the truth is that they are far more likely to suffer harm than to endanger others. We're afraid they could take over our lives. What if their challenging constellations of need, unpredictable behavior, and eruptive outbursts impede our own safe and secure lives? Our predictable and programmed congregations?

We sometimes manage to overcome those kinds of fear when considering the foster care of traumatized children. Maybe because we are confident their young brains still have time to grow and change into the "normal" ways we expect. Adults with long-standing mental health problems represent a different challenge. Can we live with difficulties that may be alleviated, but might never go away?

One older woman rejected fear when she opened her home to a person with a serious mental health problem. Her faith-filled generosity provided stable housing that helped stabilize his condition and also allowed him to provide some support for her occasional needs. Her fearlessness also provided many anxious months for her (also faith-filled) children as they waited for his erratic behaviors to subside. Courageous living is not for the faint of heart—or even sometimes for the pragmatic.

To take care of another at personal risk is not something many of us are willing to consider. Yet it is what we must do if the body is to be healthy. If we truly believe that we are one body in Christ, then the weakness or injury of any part is limiting to all. That means that the difficulties we are prone to relegate to "that individual" or "that family" are, in God's view, difficulties that are damaging to all God's people.

We can justify self-protection from Scripture, and often do. God says we are to "bear ye one another's burdens and so fulfil the law of Christ" and then tells us, within just a few lines, that "every man shall bear his own burden" (Galatians 6:2, 5 KJV). Which should we choose? Many of us pick one or the other, then justify our choice in a way that reflects our own way of life. We don't live easily with a divinely directed "both/and," maybe because it requires us to turn humbly and fearlessly to the Author to understand what applies right now. Is this moment a time to "bear ye one another's burdens" or a time to enforce "every man shall bear his own"? I'm not likely to know by myself. But God does. And happily, God is available to be asked and is willing to answer with wisdom for any who seek it.

We're also sometimes prone to accuse the person in pain when the situation requires gracious support of the person's need. Americans used to say, "God helps those who help themselves." Today, we more often hear variations of "What you think, you create" and "If you believe it, you can achieve it." Either way, the underlying belief is that suffering people deserve their pain. They have failed to do the right thing or to think the right thing, bringing difficulties down on themselves. This view is echoed in healing theories, both Christian and non-Christian, that urge sufferers to root out the failing in themselves that must underlie the illness or emotional pain.

In my early thirties, I ended up on crutches twice in a year, having managed to sprain each ankle in oddball accidents. A friend asked, "Why are you trying to avoid moving forward in your life?" I could only shake my head and continue swinging forward on my crutches.

A BIG FEAR: MAYBE THEY'RE NOT THAT DIFFERENT . . .

We live in a time when the boundary between what is real and what is imagined is just an Internet rabbit hole away. It's frightening how easily any of us can be carried into alien thought systems. We spend more time than we'd ever have expected interrogating our own sense of sanity. How can we recognize the line between what is only different and what is truly unreal? What to do when we face ideas that really don't seem sane?

Nearly a decade ago, before rampant conspiracy theories and "fake news" assertions radically undermined our sense of reality, Stanley Hauerwas suggested that the "world we call 'sane'" may be more fragile than we like to believe, and described how we become wary and fearful when we sense that fragility. To discover that even the world of those we consider stable is less solid than we hoped "makes us all the more determined to distance ourselves from those who suffer from mental illness."[9] This is not so different from the fear many of us experience when visiting the sick or dying. In their presence we are forced to remember that we, too, are mortal, and for many that reminder, too, is fearful.

THE GREATEST FEAR: I WON'T PREVENT THEIR SUICIDE

When my friend Kelly was overcome by paranoia and called me to take her home from work, I left my own job in the middle of the day. Another friend and I held her and prayed with her for hours. That day, the storm lifted from her soul.

Eighteen months later, my phone rang in the middle of the night. I stumbled to it in the deep blackness of a hurricane power outage and learned that Kelly's body had been found. She had died by suicide in the women's restroom of a restaurant hundreds of miles from her home.

Kelly's friends and church had been with her and for her as best we knew for many years. As friends, we enjoyed her ebullient spirit, prayed with her, and did our best to help her make sense of her sometimes unusual religious experiences. As friends, we could encourage her to seek professional help, but had no power to force it. And because she was an adult with some measure of self-control, she was able to behave in a way that fooled the people around her when she'd reached her point of decision. She was fine, she said that morning. She was going to work.

But she never came home. And then the call came.

It was nearly a decade before I talked about Kelly's death with our other roommate. We still had questions. Why did she kill herself? Why was she riding a bus to North Carolina? And the biggest question of all: Could we have done anything to save her?

Suicide loss is a complicated grief. It encompasses loss, self-recriminations, and sometimes even relief that a wearying relationship is finally ended—which fuels a new round of self-recrimination. Survivors are plagued by the fear that the death is their own fault. Mental health training for laypeople in the United States aims to turn as many people as possible into frontline suicide risk scanners, in confidence that we can identify the individuals at risk, move them out of harm's way, and ultimately attain a relatively recent "zero suicide" goal.[10] It requires us to believe that people can successfully discern other people's deepest, darkest thoughts just as "the LORD searches every heart and understands every desire and every thought" (1 Chronicles 28:9).

Not surprisingly, this strategy, which requires a divine level of insight from flawed humans, isn't working. The United States has trained more than two million people in Mental Health First Aid[11] and another three million in QPR (Question, Persuade, Refer) techniques,[12] and we have watched our suicide rate continue to rise. With more than three in every two hundred Americans now trained to peer into other people's minds for the warning signs of suicide, the US suicide rate has not declined. Not only is our suicide rate higher than the global average; it has risen by 33 percent since 1999, while the rate of suicide death worldwide fell by nearly the same percentage.[13]

Still, those left behind after a suicide death bear a traumatic burden of guilt. We're the kind of animal that makes sense of situations by finding cause and effect. And so we turn our questions about cause into questions of personal guilt and responsibility. Just as in generations before, we dig endlessly at memory: Did I say something unkind? Did I do something to upset? But now we have new reasons to self-accuse. We failed to use our training, or we failed to obtain training, or we failed to refer to a trained person. We give ourselves only bad choices when someone dies by suicide: either feel guilty for not having tried to help or feel guilty for having tried and failed.

Guilt and self-blame may be inevitable, but that doesn't make them truthful. The truth is, none of us ever does everything possible in any situation. We can only do what is possible within our current personal limits, which are almost always less than the optimal human contribution, which is in turn always less than the broad horizon of possibility that God sees.

Al Hsu wrote *Grieving a Suicide: A Loved One's Search for Comfort, Answers, and Hope* as he worked through feelings about his father's suicide death. Hsu is straightforward in urging others to let go of self-accusation: "Whatever the reasons might have been, our loved ones ultimately made their own choice to take their own lives. They did not do so because of us or to hurt us; their focus was on ending their own pain. We survivors can let go of our sense of guilt and responsibility for the death."[14]

SMALL BEGINNINGS: MAKE A SAFER PLACE

Aiming at fearlessness doesn't require us not to feel fear. Nor does it require us to just tough it out. Some of the best tools for beating back fear involve creating safer environments. For caregivers, that might mean establishing care teams. A congregational care team of several people is able to reduce the burden any individual will feel. Team members can train and support each other in the skills of good caregiving, perhaps using resources from an established church caregiving program[15] or from their denomination, association, or fellowship. They can also debrief difficult experiences, making it less likely that anyone will be overwhelmed by needs they don't know how to address and reassuring those who feel they've failed when a situation deteriorates.

Creating safer places for those living with mental health challenges might mean structuring the congregation to meet specific safety and security needs. As one example: congregations where small groups typically reorganize every few months are overwhelming for those who find relationship transitions difficult. But these congregations can still offer long-term activities that function as small relational groups, such as a choir or a Celebrate Recovery group. These can become safe places of trusted friendship, where people can describe difficult feelings without fear.

THE CHALLENGE

We're human. We like to feel safe. We don't like putting ourselves or our plans at risk if the risk seems avoidable. How many times have you relied on someone to do a task and then had him step out because he's just not at his best? Keeping our plans moving forward—including the plans we have for our congregations—can incline us to shy away from people and situations we can't easily predict. And people with mental health problems can be unpredictable.

Being human, we like to do well and to look well in front of others. That can mean we shy away from needless challenges. And what could be more challenging than people who are different enough that we can't always understand their motives and actions? When we don't understand a person, it's difficult to enfold that individual into our activities. It's difficult to know how to encourage and support the person.

Of course, on the flip side, those of us who live with mental health problems often don't understand you. We don't understand how you laugh so easily. How you stay in touch with so many friends and business relations. How you look down a black diamond ski slope—whether the real thing covered with snow or the metaphorical high-risk, high-reward situation—and just say, "Here goes!" We'd like to do well and look well, too. And we know by experience that we often will not succeed.

Facing difficult situations with courage is a skill we all need, whether we live with mental health challenges or are currently free of them. Discovering that I am smaller than the challenge before me is part of being human. Those of us with mental health challenges and those currently without them must all practice the same difficult discernment: Is the challenge I'm facing today too big for God to accomplish through me? Do I really need to fear this situation when I am with God? Is this challenge one I can't learn to meet? And if this challenge is truly beyond me, can I agree with God that I am not limitless? Am I willing to ask for help? Can I walk among these challenges without fear?

THE GOOD NEWS

God has walked this path before you, and God is walking this path with you. There is no need to be afraid in the presence of God.

God promises that those who follow him will "come in and go out" of the sheepfold and still be safe (John 10:9).[16] The blessing of the going out, as this metaphor suggests, is that "out" is where almost everything important happens. Out in the pasture is where sheep get most of their food. Out in the pasture is where sheep find mates and procreate. Out is where sheep find fresh air and running water and sunshine.

"In" is a safe place to rest, and rest is important. But what happens in the pasture is most of life.

We who live with mental health problems often seem restless. We're not easy to call into the fold. Some of us feel confined there. Some of us expect, at any moment, to be thrown out. The place where you feel most safe and at ease may feel less safe to us than the howling wilderness at night. At least in the wilderness, the risks come from things that everyone agrees are dangerous. In the fold, our frozen stare when faced with an unexpected question poses a risk of social ostracism that others are unlikely to understand.

Yet the challenges that those of us who live with mental health problems face can make us effective in caring for others. Suffering is its own kind of training for caregiving. John Swinton notes, "It is not insignificant that those who cared most effectively were those who had experienced suffering themselves. This highlights the importance of empathy and understanding as vital aspects of the caring process."[17]

The good news for those of us who live with mental health problems is that God has prepared us for kinds of service that others may find fearful or challenging. The good news for those who don't have mental health problems is that any suffering you have experienced acts as preparation for your own empathetic and fearless caregiving.

The Christian supporter is able to be fearless when interacting with someone very different from herself because God has taught her to "fear not." The Christian supporter can listen compassionately, even to a person who is describing what is patently unreal, because he stands with the One who is the foundation of all reality. She is ready to be present for the individual who needs to not be left alone because she stands in the place of One who has never left or forsaken her. And they are able to include those who are odd or exceptional because they have learned that God's church is not an exclusive club but a place that welcomes all who thirst and hunger. God's church is a place for those who are frightened by mental health problems, including those of us who live with fear for our own mental health.

God doesn't waste anything. We don't need to waste what God has given. We can walk without fear together with God and each other.

10

When Should a Caregiver Ask for Help?

You can't know what no one has taught you.
—MENTAL HEALTH COMMUNITY WISDOM

Twenty-some years ago, when I was a newlywed living in a new city and still new to the congregation where my husband was an elder, my new doctor changed the treatment protocol that had sustained me through more than a decade.

I had a bad reaction. This doctor's treatment strategy turned what had been effectively managed as intermittent depressions into a bipolar mania. I slammed doors, shouted at the pastor, verbally barraged the elders, and battered my husband—albeit only with a worn-out sneaker on his rear end. Such is what mania imagines to be self-control.

The congregational leadership was appalled. If I was so unhappy with the church, they said, I should find a better fit elsewhere.

I spent nearly six months searching solo, much of it in the fragile "kindling" stage when the post-manic person is always on the verge of swinging into another crisis. Then the leadership instructed my husband that we needed to be in a congregation together. He, too, should leave. Being separated from the elders who had been his closest friends was devastating.

Today, I have renewed relationships with some of that leadership team, and they regret their response. "We didn't know much about mental illnesses," they acknowledge. Nor did I at that time. If I had, I might have realized that the doctor's seemingly small change in my longtime treatment could have provoked exactly the behaviors I was experiencing. I might have been able to beg for time to recover, instead of accepting a transition out of the only community of belonging I knew in my new city.

When should you ask for help? When you don't understand what you're experiencing. When you feel incompetent to the task before you. When you don't know how to respond. Most often, that requires looking for a wise, experienced guide. Sometimes that will involve finding professional support. Even then, it almost never requires shutting a person in mental health crisis out of your congregation. You and others in the congregation can maintain supportive community with people who are struggling, even while you open a door to considering care options that are beyond your skills.

WHO CAN CAREGIVERS GO TO FOR HELP?

The best initial help will often come from someone you already know. That could be a person in your congregation, someone you know from your job, a neighbor, or a community organization member. A mental health professional may have useful information. So might a person who is living effectively with a mental health problem. These conversations must be confidential, and typically you will not disclose the identity of the person you're worried about. Your goal is to review the situation and clarify available options with someone whose insights you trust.

What people with mental health problems generally need from churches is not mental health treatment but Christian friendship and the kinds of caring that can emerge only among those committed to each other.[1] Faith communities are designed by God as places where people can belong, find meaning and purpose in life, be recognized as valued persons in the sight of God and other people, and find hope for the days to come. These kinds of caring don't require professional support. In fact, they happen most effectively when they are provided long term by nonprofessionals.

SIGNALS THAT CAREGIVERS MAY NEED HELP

Admittedly, sometimes the support needed is far beyond what the congregation can provide. My moment of bipolar mania was clearly one such time. But remember: Sending someone for additional help and shutting a person away from the help of the congregation are not the same thing. Likewise, knowing that the congregation can be a primary support and believing oneself to be the right supporter at a given moment are two different things.

Here are five clues that you might want to ask for help, whether from a professional or a wise friend:

If you feel uneasy, ask for help. Uneasiness is a warning that something is off. It might mean that you recognize subconsciously a risk you can't yet name. It can also mean that your intuition knows this moment is beyond you. Recognize this as a signal that you need help, not a sign that this person is "too much."

If you feel overly confident in how you're handling the relationship, consider at least finding a backup. Excessive confidence can be a symptom of the pride that goes before a fall (Proverbs 16:18). It's bad enough to put yourself at risk, but in this case there's also someone else to consider.

If you feel overburdened, ask for help. A person who carries a heavy load of caregiving may be skilled in giving care but may not have the time or energy for serving even one more person. Allow yourself to be the limited human being that God made you.

If your own experiences are becoming triggers to you or the other person, ask for help. Our own struggles often equip us to help others. This is covered in principle by 2 Corinthians 1:4. We comfort others with the comfort we ourselves have received and continue to receive from our loving God. Remarkably, God tells us that by having experienced God's comfort "in all our troubles," we become able to comfort others who are "in *any* trouble" (my emphasis). Our ability to share comfort isn't limited to the kinds of challenges we ourselves have faced. This can be reassuring for those who may have experienced God's comfort in grief but never depression; in fear but never panic. At the same time, your experience with similar situations may not align with what is most helpful in a particular situation.

If you are becoming caught up in the other person's experiences, ask for help. Our own past or current struggles may make us more likely to become entangled in or traumatized by someone else's challenges. This can happen when caregivers are highly empathetic; it often occurs because caregivers are attempting to support someone whose trauma is similar to an unresolved trauma of their own. My own volunteer healthcare chaplaincy does not include the psychiatric emergency center, because I don't trust my responses in that setting.

SMALL BEGINNINGS: SOME CONVERSATION GUIDES

The Christian friend can, as a nonprofessional, guide conversations in ways that help the suffering individual rediscover meaning, purpose, value, belonging, and hope. Sometimes this involves letting the person know what has been helpful to you under similar circumstances. It often involves giving the person space to explore what is and isn't helping. It always requires the patient expectation that this is just one of many conversations, not the turning point moment that will dramatically change a life. Here are a few suggestions you might consider:

Belonging: "I'm glad you reached out to me. Friends are important."

Meaning: "You must be wondering what this is all about . . . whether it could possibly have any meaning . . ."

Purpose: "I understand that you're feeling that you don't matter to anyone. I suspect you probably do matter to someone besides me. Do you ever help anyone else? Even pets?"

Value: "I hear you saying that you don't feel like you have anything to offer. If it's okay, I'd like to let you know a couple of things I value in you."

Hope: "So what's the next thing you'll be doing after we get off the phone? What are you planning for dinner?"

Questions are often more helpful than answers, probably because we often learn best by discovery. Similarly, handing off a package of Bible verses may make a person feel dismissed, but describing how God's Word carried you through an overwhelming time can be helpful. Sharing your own story of God's faithfulness helps the person see you as just another person in need of God's help. If you can offer belonging in the club of those who rely on God, and can show how you have found value, meaning, and purpose as part of that community, it's possible that there is hope for the person who is struggling today.

THE CHALLENGE

"You can't give what you don't have," we are often told. But in ministries of caring, what we often need to give is precisely what we don't have. We don't have God's love; we receive it. We don't have God's mercy; we are embraced by it. We don't have physical, emotional, relational, or spiritual wholeness; but the only God, who created us, knows what wholeness looks like for each of us, and can give each of us what is needed as we grow more nearly to the wholeness that our Creator alone can see.

THE GOOD NEWS

Assisting people who live with mental health challenges doesn't require more of any individual than God has equipped us as a people to provide. We are not responsible as individuals to perfectly direct people to good mental health. Nor are most of us called to be certified master mechanics of mental health. What we are responsible to do is continue our own journey together with those God has called to the same narrow road that leads to God. That road is broad enough to encompass all that we are and will become as we travel the many routes God assigns us on our journey: professions, companions, pastimes, families, affinities, politics, and even our own stability.

God has equipped all of us to serve those with needs. God has not fully equipped any one of us to meet all of those needs. Asking for the help we need is part of our calling. When we ask for help, we allow God to draw the body together so all parts may recognize their need for each other and all parts may be built up together in love and purpose.

Afterword

It can be hard to be a person with a mental health diagnosis in a church.

I've lived more than forty years in treatment for mental health problems, the last thirty-five of those as part of churches in three US states. Some congregations have been helpful; others less so. Overall, what I want the church to understand about our life in Christ together is the following:

- *I'm part of the body.* I may be a peculiar part, but I'm a part.
- I *have gifts to offer,* which can benefit the church, the world, or both. If the body chooses to overlook me, it has chosen to lose the use of whatever part God has designed me to be. Even if I'm as unlovely and invisible a part of the body as a bile duct, the body loses a God-essential function without me.
- I *face challenges,* most of which really aren't all that different from the challenges you face. They're experienced more deeply because of my mental health problems,

and because they come to me with strong emotions or unusual thoughts, it has taken me many years to learn how to manage my responses. I have been greatly helped by friendships with wise people who have practiced and developed the skills I need. Many of those are people without significant mental health problems, because it's hard to learn ordinary behavior from those who have yet to master it.

- *God's people and God's Word are powerful to give me and everyone life.* I gain life among God's people when I'm welcomed, given opportunities to serve in the gifts God has given, and allowed to learn human living from other humans.

- *God's people and God's Word misused are powerful to deal me death.* When you label my challenges as demons or name me as unsuited to the part of the body you lead, you cast a shroud of fear and isolation over me. Those are tools of the enemy, not my God.

- *My clinicians and peer supports know more about how to manage my illness than the church does,* and that's as it should be. I don't expect my church to know as much about cancer or kidney disease as clinicians and peers would. I just expect my church to offer me the same kinds of support it provides in all those situations. At the very least, sympathy and kindness can go a long way.

I know that people often find the thoughts and behaviors of those of us with mental health problems frightening, which can make it hard to think well about how to respond helpfully. In chapter 8, you met Captain Pete Costas of the Salvation Army, and heard about the Sunday night his service was repeatedly interrupted by a visitor with a serious mental health problem. In his response, I see five principles that are helpful when interacting with those of us who live with serious mental health problems:

1. *Ask only as much of us as is reasonable.* The young man who kept breaking into Captain Costas's sermon was unlikely to arrive at church well-clothed and behaving typically anytime soon. Nor was he ready to stop asking questions. Captain Costas only asked him to refrain temporarily from asking questions. And with great effort—actually sitting on his hands to restrain himself—the young man was able to do so. Grace doesn't expect perfection today from any of us. It anticipates perfection in the fullness of God's time.

2. *Allow us to experience ourselves as part of the body.* Captain Costas helped the impatient young man see that he was in a room full of people who also wanted to know more about God. "Where there is no vision, the people are unrestrained" (Proverbs 29:18 NASB), God tells us. Captain Costas allowed this man to see himself as part of the worshiping community, not just a disruption to it, and as part of the community, the man was able to manage his behavior.

3. *Be fearless.* The moment when you meet a person who is suffering is not the moment to begin deciding whether you are afraid to reach out. Advocates for mental health funding have made much of their case in the last two decades by presenting people with diagnoses as likely to pose dangerous threats. This is unrealistic, but it has helped fund many mental health projects. Ask yourself: Did God say "Be not afraid" except in the face of unusual behavior? Respond to people with mental health challenges as directed by God, not fear.

4. *Avoid trying to diagnose us.* Diagnostic labels, especially in the hands of those who are not professionals, have become tools for dividing the body. He's a "narcissist." She's "clinically

depressed." "They" need to get their act together—preferably with the help of paid professionals—before "we" (their church) have anything to offer. The first thing any church can offer is humility in the face of lived emotional challenges. Most of us are not diagnosticians. And at a time when specialists think that half of us in the United States will experience a mental illness in our lifetime,[1] it might be worth asking whether something that is almost as common as a cold is properly isolated to expensive professional care. Maybe God's people do have something useful to offer.

5. *Listen to us. Let God answer the cries of our heart.* Our mental health problems carry our thoughts down paths you haven't imagined. They sometimes lead us to comments and behaviors you will find peculiar. We, too, are likely to be appalled by some of our behaviors when we are again "clothed and in our right mind" (see Mark 5:15; Luke 8:35). Still, in the end, we are asking the same questions you are. Your training may not have prepared you for the way we present our inquiries, but God will speak through you—just as God's Spirit provided words to the apostles (Matthew 10:19-20) and to Captain Costas.

Our communities of faith are intended to be places where we encounter God and one another. That makes them different from our broader communities, where we often encounter loneliness, anxiety, and depression instead. In a healthy congregation, we discover meaning and purpose as we learn ways to live in accordance with God's plan for our lives. We find value as we recognize that in Christ we are already God's carefully created works of art. We experience belonging as we live together into the united purpose God has created us for. And together with each other and our God, we find hope, because that is the nature of the next day God has in store for us all.

Resource List

The number of resources available to individuals experiencing mental health challenges and to people of faith seeking to respond is growing rapidly.

Many national organizations seek to assist people with mental health problems and their families. In the places where I have lived, the supportive programs they offer to people they call mental health "consumers" have often presumed that mental health problems are disabling and that it would be remarkable to have a diagnosis and be fully employed. Since I've never been able to afford not to work, that presumption has not been helpful to me. I would generally discourage others with mental health problems from using supports that presume your incompetence, since a relatively small percentage of us are actually disabled from ordinary life by our difficulties.

Most of the resources below focus on the idea that people with mental health problems can live meaningful and valuable lives as part of our communities, including our communities of faith. Excellent free resources, including an entire mental health course designed for congregational use, are often available from international sources and are included below. Please note that URLs or other contact info may have changed.

STORIES FROM LIVED EXPERIENCE

Understanding mental health challenges from the inside can make it easier to hold hope for and share hope with those of us so challenged. Here are some favorite resources, in no particular order:

John Swinton

Finding Jesus in the Storm: The Spiritual Lives of People with Mental Health Challenges. Grand Rapids: Eerdmans, 2020. If you have only one book in your lived experience collection, this should be it. Swinton is a practical theologian whose work for decades has focused on people with disabilities, Alzheimer's, and mental health challenges. In this volume, people living with mental health conditions describe how those conditions affect and are affected by their relationship with God and their communities of faith.

Jessica Faith Kantrowitz

The Long Night: Readings and Stories to Help You through Depression. Minneapolis: 1517 Media, 2020. Kantrowitz lives with depression and chronic pain. In this and other writings, she maintains a welcoming and soothing voice that could make her this century's Mr. Rogers. "You are not alone, and this will not last forever," she assures her readers and thousands of Twitter followers.

Kathryn Greene-McCreight

Darkness Is My Only Companion: A Christian Response to Mental Illness. Ada, MI: Brazos, 2006. Greene-McCreight is an Anglican priest with bipolar disorder. This widely acclaimed volume is richly theological and focuses heavily on the resource that is our faith. Now in its second edition.

Alia Joy

Glorious Weakness: Discovering God in All We Lack. Ada, MI: Baker Books, 2019. Although Joy has two mental illness diagnoses, this memoir is less about mental health problems and more about living to God's glory through many kinds of suffering. In her life, these include poverty, sexual assault, racial discrimination, childhood leukemia, a sibling's attempted suicide, a miscarriage, and asthma, as well as bipolar disorder and generalized anxiety.

Monica Coleman

Bipolar Faith: A Black Woman's Journey with Depression and Faith. Minneapolis: Fortress Press, 2016. Coleman, a theologian, explores in her memoir the intersection of mental health problems and racial trauma, suggesting that serious mental illness across many generations was obscured by the serious trauma impacts of enslavement, war, sharecropping, alcohol abuse, and poverty.

Amy Simpson

Anxious: *Choosing Faith in a World of Worry*. Downers Grove, IL: InterVarsity Press, 2014. The award-winning author helpfully distinguishes among human fear in the face of difficulties, including spiritual battles; the culturally prevalent sin of worry; and the anxiety disorders that might be diagnosed.

RESOURCES FOR PEOPLE WITH MENTAL HEALTH PROBLEMS, THOSE WHO LOVE US, AND OUR CONGREGATIONS

Fresh Hope (https://www.freshhope.us)

Of the various support group training resources aimed at congregations, this is the only one I found that was developed by a certified peer support specialist who is also a pastor. Core to the program is helping people identify any reasons for hope and how they could take steps toward the hope they find. The groups are inclusive of those with and without diagnoses, but are rooted in the experience of those who are overcoming mental health challenges.

Grace Alliance (https://mentalhealthgracealliance.org)

Their Thrive workbook is designed for those with mental health challenges and may be used individually or in groups. The wide range of offered resources includes strategies for developing effective therapeutic partnerships between clergy and mental health practitioners.

Sanctuary Mental Health Ministries
(https://www.sanctuarymentalhealth.org)

This UK- and Canada-based organization offers a free eight-part curriculum that is a very helpful introduction to mental health recovery, including discussion of how faith and mental health intersect, mental illness diagnostic basics, stigma, principles of mental health recovery, companionship, self-care, and determining next steps for the congregation. Videos represent the lives of people who have experienced mental health challenges. Leader's guides, workbooks, and videos are included in the free subscription. A special resource, *Faith, Grief, and COVID-19*, was produced during the pandemic.

Stephen Ministries (https://www.stephenministries.org)
Stephen Ministries are not mental health–focused support programs, which made them (for me) especially valuable in providing mental health supports. Stephen Ministers provide the same kind of support to a person or family in mental health crisis that they would provide in any other challenging circumstance. The use of Stephen Ministries for care is, in itself, a tool for destigmatizing mental health problems and including the sufferer in the congregation as a whole.

Companionship Movement (Pathways to Promise)
(https://www.thecompanionshipmovement.org)
Pathways offers a three-hour Companionship training to help congregations develop caring responses to those living with mental health problems and their families, plus several instructional booklets. Companionship Ministry is a compassionate framework that seeks to establish side-by-side supportive friendships for those living with mental health problems. Its core elements are listening, sharing the journey with a person side by side, neighboring (acknowledging our common humanity), providing hospitality, and helping develop a "circle of care."

Key Ministry and the writings of Stephen Grcevich
(https://www.keyministry.org)
Grcevich is a psychiatrist who seeks to make congregations more comfortable and welcoming environments to those with various mental health challenges. As of this writing, a fourteen-part video series is available to accompany *Mental Health and the Church: A Ministry Handbook for Including Children and Adults with ADHD, Anxiety, Mood Disorders, and Other Common Mental Health Conditions.*

Trauma Healing Institute (https://traumahealinginstitute.org)
The institute is best known for the curriculum *Healing the Wounds of Trauma*. Look for the US version of the curriculum, which was originally developed to help people recover in cultures devastated by war, genocide, famine, and other trauma far more obvious than what we generally experience in the United States. The international curriculum has been field-tested since 2001 and translated into more than 150 languages.

The Shay Moral Injury Center at Volunteers of America
(https://www.voa.org/moral-injury-war-inside)
The Shay Center provides training for clergy, chaplains, and mental health and medical providers in the developing field of moral injury, a kind of trauma related to circumstances that have injured individuals at the heart of their moral identity. Theologian Rita Nakashima Brock directs the center; she founded the Soul Repair Center at Brite Divinity School, Texas Christian University.

Emotional CPR (https://www.emotional-cpr.org)
Although it is less well known than Mental Health First Aid, which is also a secular resource, Emotional CPR is based on the lived experience of people with mental health challenges. It is taught through the National Empowerment Center, whose executive director, psychiatrist Daniel Fisher, lives with a diagnosis of schizophrenia. Emotional CPR coaches help people "Connect, emPower, and Revitalize" when experiencing mental health challenges.

Mad In America (https://www.madinamerica.com)
Founded in 2012 by an award-winning medical writer, Mad In America (together with its global counterparts in Europe, South America, and the Asian-Pacific region) foregrounds the idea that drug-centered mental health care is neither adequate nor truly evidence-based. It provides research reviews by professionals and essays from those with lived experience of mental health challenges.

Canadian Mental Health Association (https://cmha.ca)
CMHA supports a wide range of mental health programs and tools, including campus and workplace mental health initiatives and training for peer support specialists. Online resources are offered in both French and English.

The books of John Swinton
Widely read among chaplaincy students, this Scottish theologian's work is grounded in his first career as a nurse to those with dementia, intellectual disabilities, and mental illnesses. *Resurrecting the Person* considers how Christian friendship changes lives. *Finding Jesus in the Storm* (also listed above) allows those with mental health problems to describe how their challenges interact with their deeply valued faith.

Amy Simpson
Troubled Minds: Mental Illness and the Church's Mission.
Downers Grove, IL: IVP Books, 2013. Simpson writes as a
person whose life has been significantly affected by a family
member's serious mental illness. For this book, she extensively
interviews both those with lived experience and others who've
experienced the diagnosed illnesses of others. Her interviews
include portraits of four congregation-based mental health
ministries in the United States.

Harold G. Koenig
Faith and Mental Health: Religious Resources for Healing.
Philadelphia: Templeton Foundation, 2005. Koenig's team at
Duke University trains many academic researchers studying the
intersection of faith and health. This 2005 volume references
earlier research and proven effective faith-based strategies.

FREE MENTAL HEALTH RESOURCES
For congregations and Christians just getting started, nothing beats quality resources that don't cost money. Here are a
few favorites:

DIY workbooks
(http://www.evworthington-forgiveness.com/diy-workbooks)
Clinical psychologist Everett Worthington is a Christian who
developed these evidence-based tools while on faculty at
Virginia Commonwealth University. Topics available include
how to develop forgiveness, humility, patience, and positivity.
Downloadable online.

The Sanctuary Course for Churches

This free eight-week course from Sanctuary Mental Health Ministries provides a solid congregational foundation in mental health issues. More details above on page 196.

Mental Health Sharables: Mind and Soul Foundation
(http://www.mentalhealthaccesspack.org/)

This UK resource offers free downloads, including more than five hundred visually appealing PDF documents about mental health, pastoral care for mental health problems, and common mental illness diagnoses.

Trauma Healing Basics from the Trauma Healing Institute
(https://www.traumahealingbasics.org)

These downloadable, plain-language resources provide simple reminders of the steps a nonprofessional can take to help a person who has experienced a traumatizing circumstance.

Welcoming Places in the Community: Perspectives from Individuals with Serious Mental Illness
(http://www.tucollaborative.org/sdm_downloads/welcoming-places-in-the-community-perspectives-from-individuals-with-serious-mental-illnesses/)

This research report and associated worksheets come from the Temple University Research Collaborative on Community Inclusion of Individuals with Psychiatric Disabilities. The included worksheet *What Makes a Welcoming Community?* is helpful to congregations seeking to understand what welcome feels like to different people.

Center for Faith and Opportunity Initiatives, *Compassion in Action: A Guide for Faith Communities Serving People Experiencing Mental Illness (2020)*
(https://www.hhs.gov/guidance/document/compassion-action)
This free downloadable resource was developed from a 2019 meeting of faith community partners convened by the Office of Faith-Based Partnerships in the US Department of Health and Human Services. It encourages congregations to leverage their strengths to support and serve those with mental health challenges, and offers suggestions, including a "What Not to Say" chart.

SUICIDE PREVENTION RESOURCES
The best suicide prevention is to find a good enough alternative to dying, at least for this very moment. Hotlines and warmlines are critical supports in crises. For those who know themselves to be prone to mental health problems, coding these numbers into your phone for easy and immediate access is a valuable part of self-care.

988
The FCC has designated 988 as the new national response number for suicide prevention in the United States. It will connect callers to one of the call centers associated with the National Suicide Prevention Lifeline. It is expected to be running by mid-2022.[1]

National Suicide Prevention Crisis Line
This US network of 163 call centers nationwide answered more than 2.2 million calls in 2018.[2] Assistance is available in English and Spanish. Call 1-800-273-8255.

Crisis Text Line
Text 741741 in the United States and Canada; 85258 in the UK; 50808 in Ireland. The line has fielded more than 4.9 million conversations since its founding in 2013.

Lifeline Chat
(https://suicidepreventionlifeline.org/chat)
The text service of the National Suicide Prevention Lifeline.

NAMI HelpLine
(https://www.nami.org/help)
In the United States, this is a valuable specialty resource if it is staffed in your state by people with lived experience of diagnosed mental illness. These "peer" staff are helpful when many would not begin to know the answer. They are also very responsive to legal concerns about mental health discrimination. Call 1-800-950-6264 or hit the Chat with Us button at the NAMI website.

THE CONGREGATIONAL REFERRAL LIST
Many organizations recommend development of a mental health provider referral list so pastors will have at hand the names of quality mental health practitioners when needed. The development and maintenance of these lists involves several potential challenges:

- *On what basis does the pastor determine the provider's quality?* Credentialing is typically used, but the success of mental health treatments depends most on the relationship established between the patient and provider. This will vary from person to person. Choosing the appropriate provider can require an individual to engage in an extended process of experimental visits to find the right match.

- *Will the congregation limit referrals to providers whose faith matches their own?* Even in large metropolitan areas, this can make for a very short list. When I lived in Wake County, North Carolina, only one psychiatrist among dozens practicing was recommended as a fellow believer among the dominant evangelical community.

- *How will insurance issues affect access to recommended providers?* Insurance providers require higher payment if the provider is out-of-network, and because of insurance hassles, many mental health practices keep themselves entirely outside the insurance system. Insurance networks also change frequently, adding another layer of complexities. Insurance issues can make an entire referral list unaffordable to a specific individual seeking help.

Referral lists are difficult to create and maintain. Making a good referral depends on skills in diagnostic and provider assessment that are often outside the pastor's area of expertise. Creating a helpful referral list also requires overcoming some significant challenges, as outlined above. And should a list be produced, when people in need are simply handed a list, they are left to navigate a very difficult process during a time when they may not be in a condition to follow through on it.

Building a good referral list may be less helpful than creating a congregational partnership to support individuals through the process of finding the right care and the period of treatment. This could happen within existing caregiving structures. One strategy would be to schedule meetings to touch base during the often lengthy and discouraging process of finding the right practitioner. Scheduled meetings during treatment can also help individuals hold confidence in God's embrace, even while various medicines are creating such dramatic changes that they're losing confidence in their own identity. This is how one congregation's Stephen Ministry supported me during difficult medication changes.

A helpful approach for creating a referral list, if one is still desired, would be to ask members of the congregation to recommend counselors and doctors they know to be helpful. This list would therefore be vetted only by the criterion of helpfulness to a familiar person. The risk of such a list is that it may include utter quacks who have seemed helpful to a known person. The big benefit is that it opens the congregational conversation about mental health by the nonthreatening tactic of asking for information. It gives leadership a way to identify some congregants who have faced mental health problems and who might be useful resources to another person in difficulties. It also creates a reason to include the words *mental health* in the bulletin or announcements several times a year. Referring to mental health problems from the front of the congregation is a helpful beginning to normalizing these challenges as part of ordinary Christian life.

In the end, the most helpful referral list may be the roster of people in the congregation who have lived with mental health challenges and are willing to share their experiences with others. God has supplied all our needs, including our need for brothers and sisters who have learned wisdom by their experiences. We can trust God in this, as in all things.

Acknowledgments

The people and places that nurture a project like this are many.

The congregation of Good Shepherd Lutheran Church, Brunswick, Maine, has embraced me and encouraged me with their questions and faithful prayers, especially pastor Rebecca Wegner, now retired; choir director and retired psychologist Sue Blakemore; retired case manager Betsy Kopyc; and attorney Patti Davis and software engineer/schoolteacher Felicity Brewer, who adopted me into their family.

The members of Redbud Writers Guild, including:

- Leslie Troutman Verner, who introduced me to Herald Press.
- Dorothy Littell Greco, who provided an extremely helpful round of initial comments on the manuscript.
- Connie Jakab, who invited me to speak on this topic during a conference she hosted.
- April Yamasaki, who touched in with encouragements along the way.

Longtime friends and encouragers:

- Amritari Martinez, whose mental health recovery includes teaching yoga six days a week, sometimes at an outpatient mental health center.
- Lianne Calvert McGregor, who has turned her own long-time recovery journey into a helpful coaching practice.
- Cecelia Barker, who I met in the only Bible study I've ever attended that prioritized building strong relationships—here we are, still friends after more than a quarter century.
- Anne Freeman: perseverance, hospitality and humility are great gifts that Anne shares as an ASL interpreter and member of the body.
- Beverly Brown, cheerleader and inviter extraordinaire, who I imagine waving her Minnie Mouse gloves to invite readers into the book.
- Heidi Smid, my former assistant editor at *The New England Christian*, whose household provided me two weeks of respite during a family crisis.
- Mary DeWitt: we shared vacations while single; now her extended family counts me in for all the holidays.

Walking buddies Ellen Maling, Karen Hefler, Sarah Brayman, and Margaret Leonard kept me from living only in my house and in my head even while we all lived at social distances because of the coronavirus.

My neighbors Linda Colwell and Jen Ortiz regularly asked after this project and helped keep me smiling through the COVID pandemic.

The Western Mass Recovery Learning Community (now the Wildflower Alliance) was there when I needed recovery supports.

My four sibs, Jon, Don, Sue, and Sarah, helped with home and auto repairs and encouraged me in cake baking, garden planting and distance walking.

My thinking has been stimulated by many sources, including ongoing great conversations at Duke Divinity School's Theology, Medicine, and Culture seminars, at the Academy of Presidential Scholars (thanks, Drs. Ellen Mandell and Christine Rafal), and online at Mad in America. Scottish theologian John Swinton, whose work I discovered about halfway through this project, was a TMC speaker.

Finally, I must acknowledge that this book might not have been written without the COVID-19 pandemic. COVID cut my commute to six feet (from the writing side to the business side of my home office); my mind was freed from FOMO to focus; and many, many people discovered for the first time that when circumstances are difficult enough, most of us experience mental health problems. When life is tough, mental health problems can be quite normal. And that knowledge can be liberating to all of us. COVID helped me, and I think others, recognize the meaning and purpose God has established for this moment, the value God has placed in us, the reality of our belonging among God's people, and the hope God has set before us all.

Thanks be to God.

Thanks be to God indeed.

Notes

INTRODUCTION

1 "Provisional Drug Overdose Death Counts," *Centers for Disease Control and Prevention, National Center for Health Statistics*, April 14, 2021, https://www.cdc.gov/nchs/nvss/vsrr/drug-overdose-data.htm.

2 Amy Simpson, "The Healing Power of Serving Others: Become a Community of Hope" (Church Mental Health Summit 2020, Hope Made Strong, online, October 10, 2020).

3 Carlene Hill Byron, "Suicide Learning from Global Perspectives." (NAMI-NC State Conference, Raleigh, NC, October 24, 2015), https://www.academia.edu/23772715/Suicide_Learning_from_Global_ Perspectives

CHAPTER 1

1 "Data and Publications," Mental Health, Centers for Disease Control and Prevention, January 26, 2018, https://www.cdc.gov/mentalhealth/ data_publications/index.htm.

2 Emily P. Terlizzi and Benjamin Zablotsky, "Mental Health Treatment among Adults: United States 2019," *NCHS Data Brief No. 380*, September 2020, https://www.cdc.gov/nchs/products/databriefs/db380 .htm.

3 Morton Kramer, "Long-Range Studies of Mental Hospital Patients: An Important Area for Research in Chronic Disease," *Milbank Quarterly* 83, no. 4 (2005): 1–12, https://www.doi.org/10.1111/j.1468-0009.2005.00422.x. Reprinted from *The Milbank Memorial Fund Quarterly* 31, no. 3 (1953): 253–64.

4 "Miltown: A Game-Changing Drug You've Probably Never Heard Of," CBC Radio, August 7, 2017, https://www.cbc.ca/radio/ondrugs/miltown-a-game-changing-drug-you-ve-probably-never-heard-of-1.4237946.

5 Jeannette Y. Wick, "The History of Benzodiazepines," *Consultant Pharmacist Journal* 28, no. 9 (September 2013): 538–48, https://pubmed.ncbi.nlm.nih.gov/24007886/.

6 Allan Horwitz, "How an Age of Anxiety Became an Age of Depression," *Milbank Quarterly* 88, no. 1 (2010): 112–38, https://www.ncbi.nlm.nih.gov/pmc/articles/PMC2888013/.

7 Although popular mental health literature still references this idea, the medical and research communities recognize it as a hypothesis still unproven after several decades. Some commentators suggest it is no more reasonable than the idea that if drinking alcohol reduces social anxiety, then social anxiety is caused by an alcohol deficiency in the brain. See an academic discussion at Kristen L. Syme and Edward H. Hagen, "Mental Health Is Biological Health: Why Tackling 'Diseases of the Mind' Is an Imperative for Biological Anthropology in the 21st Century," *Yearbook of Physical Anthropology* 171, no. S70 (November 24, 2019): S87–117, https://doi.org/10.1002/ajpa.23965.

8 Ronald C. Kessler et al., "Prevalence and Treatment of Mental Disorders, 1990 to 2003," *New England Journal of Medicine* 352, no. 24 (2005): 2515–523, https://pubmed.ncbi.nlm.nih.gov/15958807/.

9 Terlizzi and Zablotsky, "Mental Health Treatment."

10 Steven Reinberg, "U.S. Suicide Rate Climbed 35% in Two Decades," *U.S. News and World Report*, April 8, 2020, https://www.usnews.com/news/health-news/articles/2020-04-08/us-suicide-rate-climbed-35-37-in-two-decades.

11 "Suicide," National Institutes of Health: National Institutes of Mental Health, National Center for Health Statistics, January 5, 2021, https://www.nimh.nih.gov/health/statistics/suicide.

12 "Prescription Drug Overdose," National Conference of State Legislatures, December 17, 2013, https://www.ncsl.org/research/health/drug-overdose-death-rate-postcard.aspx.

13 "Provisional Drug Overdose Death Counts," Centers for Disease Control and Prevention, National Center for Health Statistics, April 14, 2021, https://www.cdc.gov/nchs/nvss/vsrr/drug-overdose-data.htm.

14 M. E. Tori, M. R. Larochelle, and T. S. Naimi, "Alcohol or Benzodiazepine Co-involvement with Opioid Overdose Deaths in the United States, 1999–2017," *JAMA Network Open* 3, no. 4 (April 1, 2020): e202361, https://jamanetwork.com/journals/jamanetworkopen/fullarticle/2764233.

15 John Henning Schumann, "I Contracted Medical Student Syndrome. You Probably Will Too," Association of American Medical Colleges, February 14, 2020, https://www.aamc.org/news-insights/i-contracted-medical-student-syndrome-you-probably-will-too.

16 In the simplest terms, OCD, or obsessive compulsive disorder, describes a person whose ordinary life is impeded by anxiety-driven repetitive or ritualistic behaviors.

17 "Mental Health: Strengthening Our Response," World Health Organization, March 30, 2018, https://www.who.int/news-room/fact-sheets/detail/mental-health-strengthening-our-response.

18 Granger E. Westberg, *Good Grief*, 35th anniv. ed. (Minneapolis: Fortress Press, 1997), 29. *Good Grief* is still in print nearly sixty years after first publication.

19 Daniel Goleman, *Emotional Intelligence: Why It Can Matter More Than IQ* (New York: Bantam Books, 1997), 70.

20 *Compact Oxford English Dictionary*, 2nd ed. (New York: Oxford University Press, 1991), s.v. "process."

21 Phillip V. Davis and John G. Bradley, "The Meaning of Normal," in *What's Normal: Narratives of Mental and Emotional Disorders*, ed. Carol Donley and Sheryl Buckley (Kent, OH: The Kent State University Press, 2000), 7–16.

22 W. Thomas Boyce, *The Orchid and the Dandelion: Why Some Children Struggle and How All Can Thrive* (New York: Alfred A. Knopf, 2019).

23 "Mental Illness," National Institutes of Health, National Institute of Mental Health, January 5, 2021, https://www.nimh.nih.gov/health/statistics/mental-illness.shtml.

24 Terlizzi and Zablotsky, "Mental Health Treatment."

25 Kirsten Weir, "Nurtured by Nature," *Monitor on Psychology*, April 2020, https://www.apa.org/monitor/2020/04/nurtured-nature.

26 JongEun Yim, "Therapeutic Benefits of Laughter in Mental Health: A Theoretical Review," *Tohoku Journal of Experimental Medicine* 239, no. 3 (July 2016): 243–49, https://doi.org/10.1620/tjem.239.243.

27 "Social Eating Connects Communities," *University of Oxford News*, March 16, 2017, https://www.ox.ac.uk/news/2017-03-16-social-eating-connects-communities.

CHAPTER 2

1 Suicide is also among the top ten causes of death in eastern Europe, central Europe, high income Asian Pacific nations, and Australasia. Mohensen Naghavi, "Global, regional, and national burden of suicide mortality 1990 to 2016: systematic analysis for the Global Burden of

Disease Study 2016," *BMJ 2019;364:l94,* February 6, 2019, https://
www.bmj.com/content/364/bmj.l94.

2 Frank Butler, conversation with author, March 14, 2020. In his retire-
ment, Butler accepted leadership roles in the Faith and Money Network
as well as Business Leaders for Sensible Priorities and Responsible Life.

3 Bianca DiJulio, Liz Hamel, Cailey Muñana, and Mollyann Brodie,
*Loneliness and Social Isolation in the United States, the United King-
dom, and Japan: An International Survey* (Kaiser Family Foundation,
2018), 9, http://files.kff.org/attachment/Report-Loneliness-and-Social-
Isolation-in-the-United-States-the-United-Kingdom-and-Japan-An-
International-Survey.

4 Vivek H. Murthy, *Together: The Healing Power of Connection in a
Sometimes Lonely World* (New York: Harper Collins, 2020), xix.

5 Vivek H. Murthy, "Work and the Loneliness Epidemic," *Harvard
Business Review*, September 26, 2017, https://hbr.org/2017/09/
work-and-the-loneliness-epidemic.

6 "U.S. Census Bureau Releases 2018 Families and Living Arrangements
Tables," US Census Bureau, November 14, 2018, https://www.census
.gov/newsroom/press-releases/2018/families.html.

7 Esteban Ortiz-Ospina, "The Rise of Living Alone: How One-Person
Households Are Becoming Increasingly Common around the World,"
Our World in Data, December 10, 2019, https://ourworldindata.org/
living-alone.

8 DiJulio, Hamel, Muñana, and Brodie, 5.

9 DiJulio, Hamel, Muñana, and Brodie, 5.

10 Veronique de Turenne, "The Pain of Chronic Loneliness Can Be
Detrimental to Your Health," UCLA Newsroom, December 21, 2016,
https://newsroom.ucla.edu/stories/stories-20161206.

11 "Facts and Statistics," Anxiety and Depression Society of America,
last modified April 21, 2021, https://adaa.org/about-adaa/press-room/
facts-statistics.

12 Jaime Ducharme, "A Lot of Americans Are More Anxious Than They
Were Last Year, a New Poll Says," *Time*, May 8, 2018, https://time
.com/5269371/americans-anxiety-poll/.

13 Fiza Pirani, "Why More Teens Are Suffering from Severe Anxiety Than
Ever Before—and How Parents Can Help," *Atlanta (GA) Journal-
Constitution*, May 2, 2019, https://www.ajc.com/news/health-med-fit-
science/why-more-teens-are-suffering-from-severe-anxiety-than-
ever-before-and-how-parents-can-help/cFlF86X6Qvn9IHqBX75jzK/.

14 "ADAA Celebrates 40 Years," Anxiety and Depression Association of America, last modified November 2020, https://adaa.org/
celebrating-40-years-2020.

15 Quoted in Johann Hari, *Lost Connections: Why You're Depressed and How to Find Hope* (New York: Bloomsbury, 2018), 14–15.

16 Allan Horwitz, "How an Age of Anxiety Became an Age of Depression," *Milbank Quarterly* 88, no. 1 (2010): 112–38, https://www.ncbi.nlm.nih.gov/pmc/articles/PMC2888013/.

17 This prescriptive behavior in congregations can promote in struggling individuals what traditional disciplines of spiritual formation called "over-scrupulosity"—excessive attention to one's own behavior in the effort to attain by one's own efforts a position of righteousness before God. Understanding over-scrupulosity could help us avoid some unhelpful approaches to counseling those in emotional pain.

18 According to psychiatrist Allen Frances, 30 percent of college students illegally obtain prescription stimulants. See Allen Frances, *Saving Normal: An Insider's Revolt against Out-of-Control Psychiatric Diagnosis, DSM-5, Big Pharma, and the Medicalization of Ordinary Life* (New York: Harper Collins Publishers, 2013), 143.

19 Daniel Rempel, "Disability, Productivity, and Living in God's Time," *Macrina Magazine*, February 1, 2020, https://macrinamagazine.com/amp/theology/guest/2020/02/01/disability-productivity-and-living-in-gods-time/. Emphasis in the original.

20 Michael Finnegan, "Poor Little Rich Kids: How Mental Health Is Affecting the Next Generation," *Campden FB*, February 24, 2017, http://www.campdenfb.com/article/poor-little-rich-kids-how-mental-health-affecting-next-generation.

21 Suniya S. Luthar and Shawn J. Latendresse, "Children of the Affluent: Challenges to Well-Being," *Current Directions in Psychological Science* 14, no. 1 (February 2005): 49–53, https://www.ncbi.nlm.nih.gov/pmc/articles/PMC1948879/.

22 Tim Newman, "Anxiety in the West: Is It on the Rise?" *Medical News Today*, September 5, 2018, https://www.medicalnewstoday.com/articles/322877.

23 Viktor Frankl, *Man's Search for Meaning* (Boston: Beacon Press, 2006), 34, 48–49.

24 Joel Achenbach, "Coronavirus Is Harming the Mental Health of Tens of Millions of People," *Washington Post*, April 2, 2020, https://www.washingtonpost.com/health/coronavirus-is-harming-the-mental-health-of-tens-of-millions-of-people-in-us-new-poll-finds/2020/04/02/565e6744-74ee-11ea-85cb-8670579b863d_story.html.

25 Jean M. Twenge et al., "Birth Cohort Increases in Psychopathology among Young Americans, 1938–2007: A Cross-Temporal Meta-Analysis of the MMPI," *Clinical Psychology Review* 30 (2010), 145–54.

26 Hari, *Lost Connections*, 117.

27 Shasta Nelson, *Friendtimacy: How to Deepen Friendships for Lifelong Health and Happiness* (Berkeley: Seal Press, 2016), 30.

28 Benjamin T. Conner, *Disabling Mission, Enabling Witness: Exploring Missiology through the Lens of Disability Studies* (Downers Grove, IL: IVP Academic, 2018), 169.

CHAPTER 3

1 Ed Stetzer, "The Church and Mental Health: What Do the Numbers Tell Us?," *Christianity Today*, April 2018, https://www.christianity today.com/edstetzer/2018/april/church-and-mental-health.html.

2 Yael Netz, "Is the Comparison between Exercise and Pharmacologic Treatment of Depression in the Clinical Practice Guideline of the American College of Physicians Evidence-Based?," *Frontiers in Pharmacology* 8, no. 257 (May 15, 2017), https://www.ncbi.nlm.nih .gov/pmc/articles/PMC5430071/.

3 When people are severely depressed, even getting out of bed may be too much for them. A gracious friend will offer and can also accept it when the offer is refused.

4 Quoted in Stetzer, "Church and Mental Health."

5 Henri J. M. Nouwen, *Gracias! A Latin American Journal* (San Francisco: Harper and Row, 1983), 19, quoted in Christine D. Pohl, *Living into Community: Cultivating Practices That Sustain Us* (Grand Rapids, MI: Eerdmans, 2012), 38.

6 "Each Winnie the Pooh Character Suffers from a Disorder: Our Childhood Has Been Ruined," *India Today*, April 20, 2016, https:// www.indiatoday.in/lifestyle/culture/story/each-winnie-the-pooh-character-suffers-from-a-disorder-tigger-a-a-milne-cma-canadian-medical-association-319011-2016-04-20.

7 Stephen A. Macchia, *Broken and Whole: A Leader's Path to Spiritual Transformation* (Downers Grove, IL: InterVarsity Press, 2015), 193.

8 Ralph Hingson and Michael Winter, "Epidemiology and the Consequences of Drinking and Driving," National Institutes of Health National Institute on Alcohol Abuse and Alcoholism, December 2003, https://pubs.niaaa.nih.gov/publications/arh27-1/63-78.htm.

9 Diana Gruver, *Companions in the Darkness: Seven Saints Who Struggled with Depression and Doubt* (Downers Grove, IL: Intervarsity Press, 2020), 33, see also 84-86.

CHAPTER 4

1 Quoted in Kristin Helmore, "A Story of Courage, Tenacity, and Hope That Has a Happy Ending," *Christian Science Monitor*, May 7, 1985, https://www.csmonitor.com/1985/0507/hklein.html.

2 Victor Frankl, *Man's Search for Meaning* (Boston: Beacon Press, 2006), 85.

3 Brad Hoefs, *Fresh Hope: Living Well in Spite of a Mental Health Diagnosis: A Wellness Workbook for Fresh Hope* (self-pub., Xulon Press, 2013), 54.

4 In 2018, a widely publicized meta-analysis of 522 trials with 116,477 participants established a clear effect for antidepressant drugs. A year later, its results were rejected by the research center whose methodology the 2018 study claimed to have used. The Nordic Cochrane Center found in 2019 that "the evidence does not support definitive conclusions regarding the benefits of antidepressants for depression in adults." Andrea Cipriani et al., "Comparative Efficacy and Acceptability of 21 Antidepressant Drugs for the Acute Treatment of Adults with Major Depressive Disorder: A Systematic Review and Network Meta-Analysis," *The Lancet*, February 21, 2018, https://doi .org/10.1016/S0140-6736(17)32802-7; then Klaus Munkholm, Asger Sand Paludan-Müller, and Kim Boesen, "Considering the Methodological Limitations in the Evidence Base of Antidepressants for Depression: A Reanalysis of a Network Meta-Analysis," *BMJ Open* 9, no. 6 (2019): e024886. https://doi.org/10.1136/bmjopen-2018-024886.

5 Edith Weisskopf-Joelson, "Some Comments on a Viennese School of Psychiatry," *Journal of Abnormal and Social Psychology* 51, no. 3 (1955): 701–3; "Logotherapy and Existential Analysis," *Acta Psychotherapeutica*, 6 (1958): 195, both quoted in Frankl, *Man's Search for Meaning*, 118.

6 The Los Angeles County Jail had become the nation's largest de facto mental health facility by the late 1990s, with roughly 3,300 diagnosed inmates. E. Fuller Torrey, "Deinstitutionalization: A Psychiatric Titanic," *Frontline*, May 10, 2005, https://www.pbs.org/wgbh/pages/ frontline/shows/asylums/special/excerpt.html. As of 2018, the three largest psychiatric care institutions in the United States were jails in Chicago, Los Angeles, and New York. Ailsa Chang, "'Insane': America's 3 Largest Psychiatric Facilities Are Jails," National Public Radio, April 25, 2018, https://www.npr.org/sections/health-shots/ 2018/04/25/605666107/insane-americas-3-largest-psychiatric-facilities-are-jails.

7 Bessel van der Kolk, "Posttraumatic Stress Disorder and the Nature of Trauma," *Dialogues in Clinical Neuroscience* 2, no. 1 (2000): 7–22, https://www.ncbi.nlm.nih.gov/pmc/articles/PMC3181584/.

8 "Frequently Asked Questions about Moral Injury," Shay Moral Injury Center, Volunteers of America, accessed March 23, 2021, https://www .voa.org/moralinjury-faq.

9 "The Sanctuary Model," Sanctuary Institute, accessed March 3, 2021, http://www.thesanctuaryinstitute.org/about-us/the-sanctuary-model/.

10 SAMHSA Trauma and Justice Strategic Initiative, *SAMHSA's Concept of Trauma and Guidance for a Trauma-Informed Approach*, HHS Publication No. (SMA) 14-4884 (Rockville, MD: 2014), 7. Available at http://store.samhsa.gov/product/SAMHSA-s-Concept-of-Trauma-and-Guidance-for-a-Trauma-Informed-Approach/SMA14-4884.

11 "Trauma Healing Basics: What Is Trauma?," Trauma Healing Institute, accessed March 2, 2021, https://www.traumahealingbasics.org/what-is-trauma.

12 The Shay Moral Injury Center of the Volunteers of America is approaching the broader issues of moral injury across the culture. It is led by theologian Rita Nakashima Brock, who previously founded the Soul Repair Center at Brite Divinity School, Texas Christian University.

13 Rosaria Champagne Butterfield, *The Gospel Comes with a House Key: Practicing Radically Ordinary Hospitality in Our Post-Christian World* (Wheaton, IL: Crossway, 2018), 57.

14 Kathryn Greene-McCreight, *Darkness Is My Only Companion: A Christian Response to Mental Illness*, rev. ed. (Grand Rapids, MI: Brazos Press, 2016), 111.

15 Stephan Pastis, *Pearls before Swine*, December 13, 2020 (Kansas City, MO: Andrews McMeel, 2020).

CHAPTER 5

1 Stanley Hauerwas, "What Have I Done? Reflections on God and Mental Illness after 'Hannah's Child,'" *ABC Religion and Ethics*, June 11, 2013, https://www.abc.net.au/religion/what-have-i-done-reflections-on-god-and-mental-illness-after-han/10099810.

2 "Friendship and Mental Health," Mental Health Foundation, August 14, 2018, https://www.mentalhealth.org.uk/a-to-z/f/friendship-and-mental-health.

3 Rosaria Champagne Butterfield, *The Gospel Comes with a House Key: Practicing Radically Ordinary Hospitality in Our Post-Christian World* (Wheaton, IL: Crossway, 2018), 108.

4 Robert Keough, "Robert Putnam on the Decline of Civic Life," *Commonwealth Magazine*, August 1, 2000.

5 National Institute of Mental Health, Office of Science Policy, Planning, and Communications Science Writing, Press, and Dissemination Branch, *Social Anxiety Disorder: More Than Just Shyness* (Bethesda, MD: National Institute of Mental Health, rev. 2016), https://www.nimh.nih.gov/health/publications/social-anxiety-disorder-more-than-just-shyness/.

6 "Social Anxiety Disorder," National Institute of Mental Health, last updated November 2017, https://www.nimh.nih.gov/health/statistics/social-anxiety-disorder.shtml.

7 "CDC Estimate on Autism Prevalence Increases Nearly 10 Percent," Autism Speaks, March 26, 2020, https://www.autismspeaks.org/press-release/cdc-estimate-autism-prevalence-increases-nearly-10-percent-1-54-children-us.

8 Simone Croezen, Mauricio Avendano, Alex Burdorf, and Frank J. van Lenthe, "Social Participation and Depression in Old Age: A Fixed-Effects Analysis in 10 European Countries," *American Journal of Epidemiology* 182, no. 2 (July 15, 2015): 168–76, https://www.ncbi.nlm.nih.gov/pmc/articles/PMC4493978/.

9 "Attending Church Is the Key to Good Mental Health," London School of Economics, August 4, 2015, https://www.lse.ac.uk/lse-health/news-events/2015/church-key-to-good-mental-health.

10 It is important to acknowledge that churches are not always safe or helpful places. The devastation posed by an abusive church leadership is briefly referenced in chapter 4 as a form of moral injury. It goes beyond the scope of this chapter.

11 John Swinton, *Spirituality and Mental Health Care: Rediscovering a "Forgotten" Dimension* (London: Jessica Kingsley Publishers, 2001), 115.

12 We often hear that stigma has decreased, but research shows a more nuanced picture. Willingness to seek and receive mental health treatment has increased, while stigma against those with mental health problems has also increased significantly. See Bernice Pescosolido, "The Public Stigma of Mental Illness: What Do We Think; What Do We Know; What Can We Prove?," *Journal of Health and Social Behavior* 54, no. 1 (2013): 1–21, https://www.ncbi.nlm.nih.gov/pmc/articles/PMC4437625/.

13 Patrick W. Corrigan, *The Stigma Effect: Unintended Consequences of Mental Health Campaigns* (New York: Columbia University Press, 2018).

14 Ed Stetzer, "The Church and Mental Health: What Do the Numbers Tell Us?," *Christianity Today*, April 2018, https://www.christianitytoday.com/edstetzer/2018/april/church-and-mental-health.html.

15 Alia Joy, *Glorious Weakness: Discovering God in All We Lack* (Grand Rapids, MI: Baker Books, 2019), 30.

16 Peter D. Kramer, "Prozac Nation? The Returns Aren't In," *Slate*, February 11, 2008, https://slate.com/culture/2008/02/charles-barber-s-comfortably-numb.html.

17 John Swinton, *Resurrecting the Person: Friendship and the Care of People with Mental Health Problems* (Nashville: Abingdon Press, 2000), 39, 48–49.

18 William Nash, "Dr. William Nash Discusses Moral Injury beyond the Military Context," Shay Moral Injury Center, Volunteers of America, January 8, 2019, https://www.voa.org/moral-injury-center/videos/dr-william-nash-discusses-moral-injury-beyond-the-military-context.

19 Vivek Murthy, *Together: The Healing Power of Connection in a Sometimes Lonely World* (New York: Harper Collins, 2020), 163–64.

20 Carolyn Hall, conversations with author, 2019.

21 Jerome A. Motto and Alan G. Bostrom, "A Randomized Controlled Trial of Postcrisis Suicide Prevention," *Psychiatric Services* 52, no. 6 (2001): 828–33, https://stanford.app.box.com/s/ewj7qr8rn9jz0ezk1gugu5cqj9cw2zeo.

22 The last example comes from Stephen Grcevich, *Mental Health and the Church: A Ministry Handbook for Including Children and Adults with ADHD, Anxiety, Mood Disorders, and Other Common Mental Health Conditions* (Grand Rapids, MI: Zondervan, 2018), 103.

23 See other examples in Grcevich, *Mental Health and the Church*, 128–35.

24 Narcissistic personality disorder is today considered to be a hard-to-treat mental health condition "driven by deep insecurity." See "Narcissistic Personality Disorder," Cleveland Clinic, June 19, 2020, https://my.clevelandclinic.org/health/diseases/9742-narcissistic-personality-disorder.

25 Tayebeh Fasihi Harandi, Maryam Mohammad Taghinasab, and Tayebeh Dehghan Nayeri, "The Correlation of Social Support with Mental Health: A Meta-Analysis," *Electronic Physician* 9, no. 9 (2017): 5212–222, https://dx.doi.org/10.19082%2F5212, quoted in The Partnership Center, Center for Faith and Opportunity Initiatives, US Department of Health and Human Services, *Compassion in Action: A Guide for Faith Communities Serving People Experiencing Mental Illness and Their Caregivers* (Washington, DC, 2020), 23, https://www.hhs.gov/sites/default/files/compassion-in-action.pdf.

26 Murthy, *Together*, 34.

CHAPTER 6

1 A good discussion of gift and exchange economies appears in chapters 1–7 of Lewis Hyde's *The Gift: Creativity and the Artist in the Modern World*, 2nd ed. (New York: Vintage Books, 2007).

2 See, for example, the description of a two-week Passover festival during King Hezekiah's reign in 2 Chronicles 30.

3 In God's grace, the nursing mother's outpoured love to her child also generates chemical changes in her body that increase the love between them. So the relationship is not just formed by her love but also helps form love.

4 John Swinton, *Resurrecting the Person: Friendship and the Care of People with Mental Health Problems* (Nashville: Abingdon Press, 2000), 205.

5 Nelson is very clear, however, that sharing good feelings and encouragement is core to quality friendships. See *Friendtimacy: How to Deepen Friendships for Lifelong Health and Happiness* (Berkeley: Seal Press, 2016), 33.

6 Swinton, *Resurrecting the Person*, 36.

7 Neil Howe, "America the Sleep-Deprived," *Forbes*, August 18, 2017, https://www.forbes.com/sites/neilhowe/2017/08/18/america-the-sleep-deprived/.

8 "Sleep and Sleep Disorders: Data and Statistics," Centers for Disease Control and Prevention, May 2, 2017, https://www.cdc.gov/sleep/data_statistics.html.

9 Stephen A. Macchia, *Broken and Whole: A Leader's Path to Spiritual Transformation* (Downers Grove, IL: InterVarsity Press, 2015), 37.

10 Cited in Christine D. Pohl, *Living into Community: Cultivating Practices That Sustain Us* (Grand Rapids, MI: Eerdmans, 2012), 56.

11 Dietrich Bonhoeffer, *Life Together (New York: Harper & Row, 1954)*, 68, quoted in Pohl, *Living into Community*, 57.

12 Ryan Sales, "Pope John XXIII and Pope John Paul II," St. Dominic Parish, April 26, 2014, https://www.stdominicparish.ca/pope-john-xxiii-and-pope-john-paul-ii/.

13 Pohl, *Living into Community*, 21.

CHAPTER 7

1 Sandro Galea, Raina M. Merchant, and Nicole Lurie, "Mental Health Consequences of COVID-19 and Physical Distancing: The Need for Prevention and Early Intervention," *JAMA Internal Medicine/Viewpoint*, April 10, 2020, https://jamanetwork.com/journals/jamainternalmedicine/fullarticle/2764404.

2 Marc Brackett, *Permission to Feel: Unlocking the Power of Feelings to Help Our Kids, Ourselves, and Our Society Thrive* (New York: Celadon Books, 2019); and correspondence with author, November 1, 2020.

3 Aundi Kolber, *Try Softer: A Fresh Approach to Move Us out of Anxiety, Stress, and Survival Mode—and into a Life of Connection and Joy* (Carol Stream, IL: Tyndale House, 2000), 172.

4 "Universal Emotions," Paul Ekman Group, last modified February 16, 2021, https://www.paulekman.com/universal-emotions/.

5 An example of the first is found in the writings of Russian Orthodox spiritual teacher Saint Theophan the Recluse, *The Spiritual Life and How to Be Attuned to It*, 4th ed. (Safford, AZ: St. Paisius Monastery, 2017), 231–33; the second represents a popular approach to practicing the Ignatian Examen; a form of it also appears elsewhere in Saint Theophan.

6 Some people on the autism spectrum have limited ability to experience feelings, and they often find human connections in different ways. At the same time, they may use a data-gathering approach to learn empathetic behaviors by observing the behavioral signals that code others' emotions. See Temple Grandin and Sean Barron, *The Unwritten Rules of Social Relationships: Decoding Social Mysteries through the Unique Perspectives of Autism* (Arlington, TX: Future Horizons, 2005), 38–46, and elsewhere.

7 *Super Soul Sunday*, season 9, episode 908, "Dr. Edith Eva Eger: The Choice," aired June 16, 2019, http://www.oprah.com/own-super-soul-sunday/dr-edith-eva-eger-the-choice.

8 Philip Yancey, *Disappointment with God* (Carmel, NY: Guideposts, 1988), 52.

9 Vivek Murthy, *Together: The Healing Power of Connection in a Sometimes Lonely World* (New York: Harper Collins, 2020), xxiii–xxvi.

10 Quoted in Adam Foulds, "Emerges What I Am: How It Feels to Be Alone," *Times Literary Supplement*, May 29, 2020, https://www.the-tls.co.uk/articles/loneliness-solitude-book-review-adam-foulds/.

11 Murthy, *Together*, 162.

12 John Swinton, *Resurrecting the Person: Friendship and the Care of People with Mental Health Problems* (Nashville: Abingdon Press, 2000), 163.

13 Christine D. Pohl, *Living into Community: Cultivating Practices That Sustain Us* (Grand Rapids, MI: Eerdmans, 2012), 64.

14 Boris Groysberg and Robin Abrahams, "What the Stockdale Paradox Tells Us about Crisis Leadership," *Harvard Business School Working Knowledge*, August 17, 2020, https://hbswk.hbs.edu/item/what-the-stockdale-paradox-tells-us-about-crisis-leadership.

15 Jerome Groopman, *The Anatomy of Hope: How People Prevail in the Face of Illness* (New York: Random House, 2005), 113–20.

16 C. Richard Snyder, *Handbook of Hope: Theory, Measures, and Applications* (San Diego: Academic Press, 2000), 25.

17 W. Thomas Boyce, *The Orchid and the Dandelion: Why Some Children Struggle and How All Can Thrive* (New York: Alfred A. Knopf, 2019), 225–26.

18 Rev. William J. Barber II, "We Must Have a Third Reconstruction," *Time*, January 21, 2021, https://time.com/5931343/william-barber-inaugural-prayer-service-sermon/.

19 Psychologist Everett Worthington at Virginia Commonwealth University uses this metaphor to explain how doing forgiveness as an act—sometimes, in his lessons, physical performances of metaphorical release—can shape the spiritual "forms" into which God can pour the emotional experience of forgiveness. See Chelsea L. Greer and Everett L. Worthington Jr., *The Path to Forgiveness: Six Practical Sections for Becoming a More Forgiving Person* (January 27, 2010), 13. Available at http://www.evworthington-forgiveness.com/diy-workbooks.

20 "Recovery and Recovery Support," Substance Abuse and Mental Health Services Administration, April 23, 2020, https://www.samhsa.gov/find-help/recovery.

CHAPTER 8

1 Maj. Pete Costas, conversations and email with author, 2008, 2021.

2 Thomas Jefferson to John Adams, October 28, 1813, available at "The Correspondence of Thomas Jefferson by Subject," School of Cooperative Individualism, modified June 9, 2018, https://www.cooperative-individualism.org/jefferson-thomas_correspondence-aristocracy-of-talent-1813.htm.

3 Michael Sandel, "Does Meritocracy Destroy the Common Good?" (lecture, Virtual Stated Meeting of the American Academy of Arts and Sciences, online, August 24, 2020).

4 Katie Jones, "Ranked: The Social Mobility of 82 Countries," *Visual Capitalist*, February 7, 2020, https://www.visualcapitalist.com/ranked-the-social-mobility-of-82-countries/.

5 "Peace Child—Papua New Guinea: A Story That Impacted World Missions," *Renewal Journal*, May 8, 2019, https://renewaljournal.com/2019/05/08/peace-child-png-a-story-that-impacted-world-missions/.

6 Pastor Sanghoon Yoo, "Diversity and Trauma-Informed Ministry" (lecture, Church Mental Health Summit 2020, Hope Made Strong, online, October 10, 2020).

7 Some people with disabilities are inventors, especially of adaptive devices they need, and many important technologies have grown from research to support people with disabilities. Some of the first research on voice-command personal computers was done at the Massachusetts Institute of Technology at the request of visually impaired musician

Stevie Wonder, who wanted to be able to use these then-new tools. One of my neighbors in Cambridge was on this research team in the late 1970s.

8 Stanley Hauerwas, "What Have I Done? Reflections on God and Mental Illness after 'Hannah's Child,'" *ABC Religion and Ethics*, June 11, 2013, https://www.abc.net.au/religion/what-have-i-done-reflections-on-god-and-mental-illness-after-han/10099810.

9 Stanley Hauerwas, *God, Medicine, and Suffering* (Grand Rapids, MI: Eerdmans, 1990), 35, 62.

10 In 2015, one in eight American adults used a benzodiazepine that had been prescribed for such conditions as anxiety, insomnia, panic disorder, and seizure disorders. Those commonly prescribed include Valium, Xanax, Ativan, Klonapin, Restoril, and Librium. "Prevalence of Benzodiazepine Use 12.6 Percent in the United States," *Psychiatry Advisor*, January 3, 2019, https://www.psychiatryadvisor.com/home/topics/anxiety/prevalence-of-benzodiazepine-use-12-6-percent-in-the-united-states/.

11 Philip J. Cowen and Michael Browning, "What Has Serotonin to Do with Depression?," *World Psychiatry* 14, no. 2 (2015): 158–60, https://www.ncbi.nlm.nih.gov/pmc/articles/PMC4471964/.

12 Kathryn Greene-McCreight, *Darkness Is My Only Companion: A Christian Response to Mental Illness*, rev. ed. (Grand Rapids, MI: Brazos Press, 2016), 185.

13 Todd Fonseca, "Lying for Success," The Leadership Lab, accessed January 10, 2021, https://theleadershiplabmn.com/?p=758.

CHAPTER 9

1 D. W. Griffith's 1909 silent short *The Maniac Cook* replaced the woodlands witch of fairy tales with a cook who tried to shove a child into the oven. This film is referenced by Steven H. Hyler in "Stigma Continues in Hollywood," *Psychiatric Times* 20, no. 6 (June 1, 2003), https://www.psychiatrictimes.com/view/stigma-continues-hollywood.

2 Statistically, people with mental health problems are more likely to be the victims of violence than its perpetrators. See Heather Stuart, "Violence and Mental Illness: An Overview," *World Psychiatry* 2, no. 2 (2003): 121–24, https://www.ncbi.nlm.nih.gov/pmc/articles/PMC1525086/.

3 Emma E. McGinty, Alene Kennedy-Hendricks, Seema Choksy, and Colleen L. Barry, "Trends in News Media Coverage of Mental Illness in the United States: 1995–2014," *Health Affairs* 35, no. 6: *Behavioral Health* (June 2016): 1127, 1128, https://doi.org/10.1377/hlthaff.2016.0011.

4 In the twenty-first century, psychiatric medications are rarely called addictive, but many cause what are called "discontinuation effects," including the raging headaches, vomiting, and dry heaves we associate with addiction. Medications with recognized discontinuation effects include the benzodiazepines prescribed, in 2015, to one in eight Americans, often for anxiety.

5 Almost all of the items in this list reference moments in my own experience of being treated with twenty-two different psychiatric medicines over four decades.

6 Ironically, on a recent personality profile I scored significantly above average on "conventionality." Apparently, I try really hard to appear ordinary, which makes it more remarkable that people consistently conclude I'm not.

7 Today researchers say that the average reduction in lifespan is between ten and twenty-five years. The reduced lifespan is attributed to a combination of factors, including medication side effects and lower quality medical treatment because of stigma. See "Information Sheet Premature Death among People with Severe Mental Disorders," World Health Organization, accessed March 23, 2021, https://www.who.int/mental_health/management/info_sheet.pdf.

8 Meagan Phelan and Natasha Pinol, "Infants Learn Better When Something Surprises Them," *American Association for the Advancement of Science*, April 2, 2015, https://www.aaas.org/news/science-infants-learn-better-when-something-surprises-them.

9 Stanley Hauerwas, "What Have I Done? Reflections on God and Mental Illness after 'Hannah's Child,'" *ABC Religion and Ethics*, June 11, 2013, https://www.abc.net.au/religion/what-have-i-done-reflections-on-god-and-mental-illness-after-han/10099810.

10 "Zero Suicide" is the name of a self-admittedly aspirational framework for mental health outcomes adopted by several US and UK healthcare systems since 2012. Its strategies specifically aim to avoid suicide death in the clinical outcomes for those receiving medical or behavioral healthcare. It targets clinical interventions and focuses on the importance of clinical care in suicide prevention.

11 "U.S. Reach," Mental Health First Aid U.S.A., August 24, 2020, https://www.mentalhealthfirstaid.org/algee-ometer/.

12 Dana Zavala, QPR Institute, email correspondence with author, January 21, 2021.

13 Katelyn Newman, "Study: Suicide Rates Decline Globally while U.S. Rate Rises," *U.S. News and World Report*, February 9, 2019, https://www.usnews.com/news/best-countries/articles/2019-02-07/global-suicide-rate-declines-while-us-rate-rises-study-finds.

14 Quoted in Jamie D. Aten, "Grasping the Complicated Grief of a Suicide: An Interview with Dr. Al Hsu on Grief and Trauma for Suicide Survivors," *Psychology Today*, June 16, 2020, https://www.psychology today.com/us/blog/hope-resilience/202006/grasping-the-complicated-grief-suicide.

15 Stephen Ministries or Pathways to Promise would be among these.

16 The word *saved/safe* is handled differently by different translators, sometimes focusing on how Jesus has "saved" us from harm (most translations) and sometimes on how we are kept "safe" (Phillips, and a translator's annotation to the New International Version).

17 John Swinton, *Spirituality and Mental Health Care: Rediscovering a "Forgotten" Dimension* (London: Jessica Kingsley Publishers, 2001), 126.

CHAPTER 10

1 In Durham, North Carolina, where I lived and worked for several years, a prominent Black congregation opened an in-house counseling center staffed by a licensed professional. This supplemented, but did not displace, existing congregational care structures. It addressed mental health access disparities that limited access to care and a well-founded historic distrust of many medical institutions by offering easy access to care from people known to be safe.

AFTERWORD

1 Anticipated rates of mental illness diagnoses keep rising, as noted in chapter 1. The 50 percent figure is from the US Centers for Disease Control in 2018; by comparison, in 2001, the World Health Organization expected only a quarter of the world's population would experience a mental health disorder. See "The World Health Report 2001: Mental Disorders Affect One in Four People," WHO, September 28, 2001, https://www.who.int/news/item/28-09-2001-the-world-health-report-2001-mental-disorders-affect-one-in-four-people.

RESOURCE LIST

1 Colin Dwyer, "FCC Approves Plan For 3-Digit Suicide Prevention Number Similar to 911," NPR, December 13, 2019, https://www.npr.org/2019/12/13/787753893/fcc-approves-plan-for-3-digit-suicide-prevention-number-like-911.

2 Dwyer.

The Author

Carlene Hill Byron is a fundraiser and communicator for nonprofits that serve people with disabilities and other profound life challenges. The former editor of *New England Church Life* and *The New England Christian* (publications of Vision New England and the Evangelistic Association of New England), she is a spiritual wellness volunteer in the MaineHealth hospital system and is active in her Lutheran church. She has been medically treated for depression or bipolar disorder since the age of nineteen, with doctors attempting more than twenty different medications to contain her symptoms. She taught NAMI's Family to Family course for eight years and spoke at the NAMI North Carolina state conference about effective global alternatives to the US model of suicide prevention. Find her online at The Mighty, Mad in America, *The Redbud Post*, and The Church and Mental Illness.